Remaking the Balkans

CHATHAM HOUSE PAPERS

The Royal Institute of International Affairs, at Chatham House in London, has provided an impartial forum for discussion and debate on current international issues for 75 years. Its resident research fellows, specialized information resources, and range of publications, conferences, and meetings span the fields of international politics, economics, and security. The Institute is independent of government.

Chatham House Papers are short monographs on current policy problems which have been commissioned by the RIIA. In preparing the papers, authors are advised by a study group of experts convened by the RIIA, and publication of a paper indicates that the Institute regards it as an authoritative contribution to the public debate. The Institute does not, however, hold opinions of its own; the views expressed in this publication are the responsibility of the author.

CHATHAM HOUSE PAPERS

Remaking the Balkans

Christopher Cviic

PINTER

THE ROYAL INSTITUTE
OF INTERNATIONAL
AFFAIRS

Pinter
A Cassell Imprint
Wellington House, 125 Strand, London WC2R 0BB, United Kingdom

First published in Great Britain in 1991 by Pinter Publishers Limited

Revised edition published in 1995

© Royal Institute of International Affairs, 1991, 1995

British Library Cataloguing in Publication Data
A CIP catalogue record for this book is available from the British Library

ISBN 1-85567-295-2 (Paperback)
    1-85567-294-4 (Hardback)

Typeset by Koinonia Limited
Printed and bound in Great Britain by
Biddles Limited, Guildford and King's Lynn

Contents

Maps

Preface to the first edition

The idea of writing a Chatham House Paper on the Balkans was suggested to me in the spring of 1990 by William Wallace, the then Deputy Director and Director of Studies at the Royal Institute of International Affairs. I doubted whether, at a time when momentous changes were taking place in the better-known Central Europe and the Soviet Union, there would be interest in a work on the Balkans. But he persuaded me that there would be and I accepted his invitation to write such a study. In the event it proved to be a prescient idea on his part.

After William Wallace's departure from the Institute at the end of 1990 to take up a post at St Antony's College, Oxford, the idea of a Chatham House Paper on the Balkans continued to be supported and encouraged by Jonathan Stern, the Acting Director of Studies. Others at the Royal Institute of International Affairs to whom I owe particular thanks for support and encouragement are Pauline Wickham, the Head of Publications, and Neil Malcolm, Head of the Soviet Programme.

I am much indebted to all those other colleagues at the Institute and friends outside who attended the two study groups and provided information and helpful comment on the manuscript, in many cases in writing. Here I must particularly mention Liliana Brisby, Richard Crampton, Richard Davy, Kenneth Duke, Jonathan Eyal, Peter Ferdinand, George Fodor, James Gow, Ja..et Gunn, Sir Reginald Hibbert, Roland Jovanovic, Anne Lane, Karl Lavrencic, Michèle Ledic, Margie Lindsay, Malcolm Mackintosh, David Madden, Branka Magas, Neil Malcolm, Charles Meynell, James Pettifer, Philip Robins, Libor Roucek, George Schöpflin, Gerald Segal, Geoffrey Stern, Trevor Taylor, Helen Wallace and David Wedgwood Benn. I must emphasize, however, that the opinions expressed here are my own, personal ones. Vladimir Pavlinic produced the maps, which should greatly assist in understanding the historical detail.

I am grateful to many other colleagues at the Institute, and particularly to staff in the two libraries. My special thanks are due to Shyama Iyer, the Soviet Programme Assistant, who was responsible for the organization of the study groups, the distribution of the manuscript and other important tasks; and to Margaret May of the Publications Department for her work on the editing and the production of the book. Lysèle Lathia, the Institute's Computer Manager, taught me how to use a word-processor and supported me generously during my long learning process. Last but by no means least, I acknowledge a very special debt of gratitude to Lieselotte Duvivier, my colleague on *The World Today*, who so willingly took many burdens off me during the rather hectic weeks when I was writing this study.

This work draws upon my postgraduate research in modern Yugoslav history many years ago at St Antony's College, Oxford, and the more recent experience, from 1969 to 1990, of reporting and analysing East and Central European affairs as a staff correspondent for *The Economist*.

London, July 1991   Christopher Cviic

Preface to the Italian edition

For the Italian edition, Chapters 5 (Turmoil in Yugoslavia) and 6 (A New Balkanscape?) have been substantially rewritten to take account of events that have taken place since this book was published. There are only a few minor changes in the earlier chapters.

London, February 1993   C. C.

Preface to the second English edition

For this edition, Chapters 5, 6 and 7 have been thoroughly rewritten. These chapters were read by Dr James Gow, of King's College, London, who made a number of helpful suggestions. A few minor changes have been made in the earlier chapters. The bibliography has been updated.

London, April 1995   C. C.

Chapter 1

Introduction

With monotonous regularity, and some justification, writers on the Balkans had for years since 1945 been echoing a famous film title: *Im Balkan nichts Neues* ('All Quiet on the Balkan Front'). The thesis of this study is that this had not been true even before the end of the Cold War and the dramatic retreat of Soviet power from Europe. Much had been happening in the Balkans under the surface even before 1989–90, but momentous changes (sadly, not all of them for the better) that have taken place there since, not least in the war-torn region of former Yugoslavia, justify a different caption. It is *Im Balkan viel Neues*: indeed most people feel that there is too much news from the Balkans these days.

What, then, is new in the region? Not, surely, its latest bout of fragmentation (or 'Balkanization') in the wake of Yugoslavia's violent break-up in 1990–91? 'Balkanization' is, by definition, nothing new in the Balkans. No, the really new thing is that at the end of the 1980s the peoples of the Balkans had found themselves – probably for the first time in their history – on their own, with no external powers trying to impose their will either on the region as a whole, or on any parts of it. The upheavals that have been taking place there (particularly the war in ex-Yugoslavia) are not being caused by external forces, as always happened in the past, but are occurring as a result of pressure from within, exerted by indigenous forces.

This study analyses some of the changes that have been taking place in the Balkans and suggests possible directions in which they may take the region. The countries addressed are Albania, Bulgaria, Romania and the successor states of former Yugoslavia: Bosnia and Hercegovina, Croatia, Macedonia, Montenegro, Serbia and Slovenia (two of those, Montenegro and Serbia, call themselves the Federal Republic of Yugoslavia).

Apart from the fact that those states are all situated wholly or partly in

1

the Balkans, they have all, until quite recently, lived under communist rule – unlike the other two Balkan states, Greece and Turkey. Neither of those two is considered in depth in this study. This is because each enjoys an ambiguous status. Greece, halfway between the Balkans and Western Europe, is a member of Nato and the European Union on the one hand, but is also deeply involved in Balkan politics and in various intra-Balkan projects. Turkey, likewise, is a Nato member (though remaining so far only an aspirant to Union membership); its history and geographical position, however, also give it an important stake both in the Balkans and in the Middle East.[1]

No analysis of the present situation makes sense without an idea of what has led up to it – particularly how the attempt of the post-1945 communist rulers at appropriating ('communizing') nationalism ended up with communism being nationalized, and how this aggravated still further the old problems the communists had inherited. This recent historical background is provided in Chapters 2 and 3. Chapter 4 deals with the dismal economic legacy of the communist era.

The fact that that legacy can now be tackled is due to the ending of the Cold War in 1989–90, which resulted in a strategic downgrading of the Balkans in East–West relations. With the release of the external corset that had gripped the whole of Eastern and Central Europe, including the Balkans, throughout the whole Cold War era, many long-suppressed national aspirations have pushed themselves up to the top of the political agenda. This is particularly true of former Yugoslavia. Chapter 5 looks at the reasons for the war there and its possible outcome. Chapter 6 discusses the implications of the changes now taking place in the Balkans for individual governments as well as for the European Union, the Council of Europe, NATO, the United Nations and other institutions.[2] Finally, Chapter 7 offers some ideas about the future shape of the Balkans.

If this study appears to be too 'Yugocentric', then that is partly because it is written by a Croat from former Yugoslavia (living in Britain since 1954), but also, and even more, because Yugoslavia has been the epicentre of the political earthquake still shaking this whole quake-prone area. Fortunately, despite the tragic course of events there since 1990–91, it is at least still highly unlikely that another world war will be sparked off by any of the current disputes, however bloody and nasty. But, as the following pages attempt to demonstrate, one thing is certain: the Balkans will continue to matter in a variety of ways to Europe and the rest of the world, and therefore deserve close outside attention.

Chapter 2

Communists as nationalists

On the face of it, the introduction of communist rule in the Balkans after 1945 represented a fundamental break with the past. The area's new rulers, in line with the ideas of Marx, Engels and Lenin, proclaimed their allegiance to the principle of 'proletarian internationalism' as the antithesis of the nationalism that had pervaded Eastern Europe under the prewar regimes. What actually happened was that even in the new power context, within the limits imposed by Soviet control, these supposedly internationalist-minded leaders continued to pursue the traditional national objectives of their individual countries.

The difference was that the pre-communist rulers were free to express their patriotism and, indeed, found it advantageous to flaunt it – it made them more popular with their own people. Their communist successors did not have this freedom: if they wanted to play the national card, they had to do so discreetly, in code, as prescribed by communist protocol.

One of the most important rules was that, whatever happened in practice, appearances had to be preserved. There was a good reason for this. To manipulate nationalism in a pragmatic way was one thing – and was broadly acceptable. To espouse nationalism openly was not, because it involved the risk of undermining the Marxist-Leninist ideology, the basis of all the communist regimes' claim to legitimacy. None of the communist leaders dared take that risk. Thus, though the practice had in effect become pure *Realpolitik*, not significantly different from that in the pre-communist era, it continued to be pursued in a communist guise.

For example, the idea that class was the basic category of domestic as well as international politics (expressed in the principle of 'proletarian internationalism') continued to be upheld. Within multinational Yugoslavia, the safely Marxist equivalent to 'proletarian internationalism' was

3

the principle of *bratstvo i jedinstvo* ('brotherhood and unity'). This satisfied the unwritten rule, observed by members of the Soviet bloc and non-aligned Yugoslav communists alike, that where ideological compromises had to be made, the necessary 're-positioning' had to be kept within the broad Marxist confines. Later on, as individual communist leaders felt more and more compelled to broaden the base of their support, nationalism became effectively 're-legitimized' in one communist-ruled country after another. Internationalist 'class' rhetoric was increasingly discarded in favour of an open appeal to national sentiment.

All this was ironic, perhaps, but hardly surprising. In the Balkans, as in the whole of Eastern and Central Europe, communism never stood a chance of bypassing, let alone supplanting, nationalism. It is not difficult to see why. Nation rather than class has been the main political category throughout the region's recent history and still is today. This is no temporary aberration but the result of centuries of experience.

Old nations, new states

The peoples of Eastern and Central Europe, including of course those of the Balkans, are old nations, many of which had once lived in states of their own. But this (often lovingly embellished) 'golden' era of independent statehood was followed by subjection to foreign rule, in some cases lasting many centuries. The four dynastic empires which between them ruled Eastern and Central Europe – the Austrian, the Prussian, the Ottoman and the Russian – were all hostile to the idea of the national state, so independent statehood had to be fought for and was gained (or regained, as those concerned would see it) by most of those nations only recently – by some as late as the end of the First World War. The political map of Eastern and Central Europe still reflects the order imposed in the aftermath of that war by the victorious Entente powers: Britain, France, Italy and the United States. That order was enshrined in a series of peace treaties – the best known of which, signed in June 1919 at Versailles, gave its name to the whole of the post-1918 settlement in Europe.

These peace treaties left much 'unfinished business' behind. The principle of national self-determination, affirmed by President Woodrow Wilson in his famous Fourteen Points of January 1918 and adopted as one of the Entente's war aims, was not fully implemented. Millions were left separated from their 'home nation'. Not all the nations of Eastern and Central Europe which aspired to independent statehood achieved it at that time. But the aspiration lived on and is still there, in some cases felt

Map 1 The Balkans in 1815

© Vladimir Pavlinic, 1991

BAVARIA

AUSTRIA

AUSTRIAN EMPIRE
Vienna

HUNGARY
Budapest

UKRAINE

BESSARABIA

MOLDAVIA

DOBRUDJA

WALLACHIA
Bucharest

BLACK SEA

VENETIA

CROATIA
Zagreb

BOSNIA

Belgrade

SERBIA

Sarajevo

O T T O M A N

MONTE-
NEGRO

BULGARIA

Constantinople

E M P I R E

ADRIATIC SEA

GREECE
Athens

AEGEAN SEA

miles 0 100 200 300 400 500

·········· Empire borders

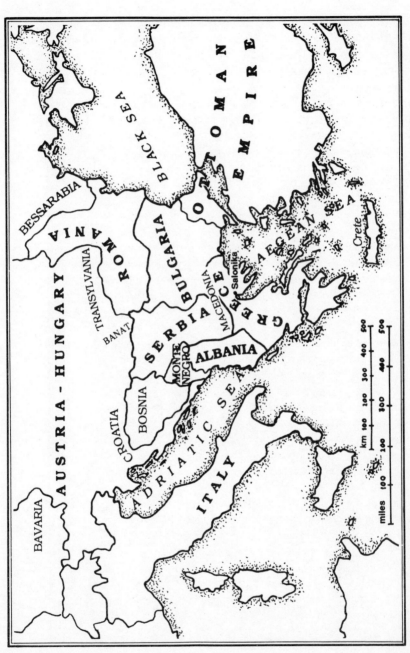

© Vladimir Pavlinic, 1991

Map 2 The Balkans in 1918

even more passionately and supported more broadly today than in the post-1918 period. Why is there still this striving for – indeed, to many Western eyes, obsession with – independent statehood? And now, of all times, when Western Europe, for example, is moving in the opposite direction, towards greater integration?

The answer lies in the East and Central European peoples' unique historical experience. In Western Europe, most of the major nations have for generations now felt secure in their identity within their established nation-states. By contrast, insecurity has been the rule in Eastern and Central Europe, and particularly in the Balkans. All the nations of that region have at some time in the past (and especially the recent past) seen their national identity, language and historical culture threatened. The old empires were by no means perfect, but the national states that followed them were almost invariably worse.

The Habsburg empire, in fact, operated on the principle of upholding the historic rights of established states. These rights included broad religious and national toleration. The introduction of the Patent of Toleration by Emperor Joseph II in 1781 enshrined an already existing practice.

Under the Ottoman empire, there existed in the Balkans the so-called *millet* system of semi-autonomous religious-national communities. The Muslim *millet* embraced no unified territory nor any homogeneous ethnic group or people of the same political and legal status. It held a position of superiority over the others because it was the only one which shared the religion and the laws of the ruling Ottoman class and its material aid. The non-Muslims were free to organize their religious, legal and educational institutions, but only from their own resources. In that sense the system held the non-Muslims back, but at the same time it enabled them to preserve their ethnic and religious identity under the leadership of the church. In the Ottoman empire this meant the Orthodox church, which the rulers found a comfortable partner and, very important, a useful Christian counterweight to the Roman Catholic church, that strong and active supporter of Europe's resistance to Ottoman invasions. That was how religion and identity became inextricably linked, and how the Orthodox church assumed its extremely important role in the public life of the individual Balkan nations.

The real threat to national identities came in the last decades of these two empires: in the Habsburg empire the Slavs felt threatened by the newly awakened German and Hungarian nationalism, and in the Ottoman empire the non-Turks saw as the main threat the Young Turks, who were looking for ways of creating a modern Ottoman identity. Moreover, in the more confined space of some of the new nation-states established after both empires broke up, minorities became exposed to a variety of dangers – from discrimination and assimilation to expulsion or even physical annihilation. Indeed, for some nations, such as the Albanians or the Macedonians, predatory neighbours not all that much bigger or more numerous than themselves have proved more deadly than the old empires ever were. The threat to the national identity of such peoples still exists today. Not surprisingly, this has helped to strengthen the bonds linking members of each individual nation to one another at the expense of class and ideological or even religious bonds. This has always posed special problems for universalist ideologies – such as communism, for example.

Marx's error

In their Communist Manifesto, Marx and Engels wrote, 'The workers have no country.' Being political realists, they accepted that the proletarian revolution would occur within a national framework, within individual states. But they did not see nations continuing after the revolution. 'National differences and antagonisms between peoples are vanishing gradually from day to day,' the Manifesto declared, and 'the supremacy of the proletariat will cause them to vanish still faster.'[3] Marx and Engels relegated the question of nationality to merely peripheral status even though it remained an important issue, for example, in Germany and Italy, which had still not achieved unification. Marx and Engels placed their hopes in the internationalist class-consciousness of Western Europe's industrial proletariat. Their calculations were put to the test in the First World War and proved wrong: the socialist parties in Western Europe voted almost unanimously for the credits needed by their 'bourgeois' governments to prosecute what any Marxist worth his salt would have designated – as Lenin did – an imperialist war.

In Central and Eastern Europe, by contrast, the socialists, however hard they tried, were never able to sidestep, let alone ignore, the 'national factor'. There was a good reason for this. As the ideology of socialism began to spread, national feeling grew in strength among the diverse peoples of the Russian and Habsburg empires and in the new states arising out of the crumbling Ottoman empire. The socialists of the Habsburg empire, whether they liked it or not, were obliged to take into account the national aspirations of the peoples they were working amongst. In the relatively democratic conditions that prevailed there, socialists had to compete for votes like everybody else. Universal franchise and the secret ballot had been achieved in the Austrian half of the empire by 1907, and cautious democratization was beginning to take off in the Hungarian half as well. The situation forced the socialists to allow for national party organizations. Thus, by the beginning of the twentieth century there were in the ramshackle Habsburg empire separate social democratic parties for the Bosnians, Croats, Czechs, Italians, Poles, Romanians, Slovenes and Romanians, as well as the German- and Hungarian-speaking population. Not surprisingly, socialist leaders in Austria-Hungary, such as Otto Bauer and Karl Renner, devoted much energy to devising ways of resolving the empire's ethnic conflicts.

The national question also posed problems for socialists in the Russian empire. But the conditions here were far more repressive. As a small, conspiratorial party made up of professional revolutionaries, Lenin's Bolsheviks did not have to make concessions to national sentiment. There were no votes that needed to be chased. The Bolsheviks could – and did – appeal to national sentiment in their propaganda in Russia before the First World War but only as a tactical expedient, without ever 'legitimizing' it. Lenin saw that nationalism could be used, in certain circumstances, to aid the cause of the revolution. But Bolshevik support for national causes had to be 'strictly limited to what is progressive in such movements'.[4]

It was entirely in this light that Lenin saw the right of a nation to 'self-determination'. There were certain conditions under which separation of a nation from the state was 'progressive' and others under which it was not. The crucial point was that it was the party which decided what was and was not progressive. Lenin shrugged off the objections of those like Rosa Luxemburg who argued that the principle of self-determination for non-Russian nationalities would, for example, deliver Poland to the control of the landlords and the bourgeoisie, and bring the Muslim population in Central Asia under the thumb of the feudal chiefs and religious leaders. What mattered to Lenin was the immediate need: the party should be able to mobilize the powerful appeal of nationalism against the tsarist state. Later on, in power, the victorious proletariat (or, rather, the party on its behalf) would judge demands for self-determination in the light of the broader, 'class' interest. And so it proved.

The federal system created under Lenin and perfected under Stalin was merely a façade covering a monolithic, centralized state. The Soviet system paid lip-service to equality for all the nations and provided for the preservation of national cultures and languages, but only to the extent that these supported Soviet, not national, policy aims. Even where local nationals held political office in the republics and other territories of the federation, Moscow always exercised absolute control – usually through the device of having a Russian as a second-in-command. It continued to pursue a long-term, though never openly declared, policy of Russification, sometimes openly stressing and at other times playing down the theory of the ultimate amalgamation of nations.

Comintern and the Balkans

In the period before the Second World War, communist parties in the Balkans were operating under several handicaps. One was that, being 'subversive' and revolutionary, they were subject to intense police pressure and forced to work in conditions of illegality. This made them even more dependent on, and constrained by, the line laid down by the Communist International (Comintern) in Moscow. The Comintern's policy was guided by the strategic and tactical interests of the Soviet state. Local political considerations were taken into account but played only a secondary role. In some cases, the Comintern's line made the local communist parties' task of winning support among their fellow-nationals easier, in others more difficult.

For example, Romania's Communist Party had a particularly hard time of it. Its main political handicap was that, because of its dependence on the Soviet Union, a country seen by most Romanians as a hostile neighbour, it was regarded by the population at large as 'anti-national'. This was perhaps inevitable in a country which had done well out of the First World War and was worried that its neighbours might seek to deprive it of its territorial gains (Transylvania, a part of Banat and northern Bukovina from Austria-Hungary; southern Dobruja from Bulgaria; and Bessarabia from Russia). The party was further damaged in the eyes of the Romanian population because (for important historical reasons) it largely comprised Jews, Hungarians and members of other minorities, rather than ethnic Romanians.

For a party already branded as an agent of a foreign power, the annexation of Bessarabia by the Soviet Union in 1940 and its amalgamation with what was then known as the Moldavian Soviet Republic was nothing short of a disaster. Comintern discipline prevented the Romanian Party from opposing the annexation, thus putting it even more at odds with the rest of the nation. It is not surprising in the circumstances that a strongly nationalist and recently humiliated country actually welcomed the Romanian government's decision to join the war against the Soviet Union on Hitler's side in 1941. The war enabled Romania not only to regain Bessarabia but also to annex extra territories (including Odessa) in the east which had never been Romanian. The area was called Transnistria and placed under a Romanian governor. This was Hitler's compensation to Romania for its loss of northern Transylvania, which had been 'awarded' to Hungary in August 1940 by Germany and Italy. In August 1944, when King Michael's coup brought Romania over to the Allies' side, the Romanian Communist Party had fewer than a thousand members. It could hardly have been otherwise: the party had nothing significant to contribute to what most Romanians, rightly or wrongly, considered as the most important item on the national agenda.

The Balkan Federation plan
Another example of the impact on the Balkan communists of the Comintern's policies was its advocacy in the 1920s and early 1930s of a Balkan Federation to replace Yugoslavia and other surrounding national states. Yugoslavia was a pillar of the French-backed cordon sanitaire in Eastern Europe, which was anti-German but also anti-communist.

The Comintern's plan was popular in *Bulgaria*. The reasons were obvious: there was widespread resentment over the loss to Yugoslavia after 1918 of the bulk of Macedonia, regarded by Bulgarians as their land, and over the consequent influx of large numbers of refugees from the so-called Vardar Macedonia, including Skopje, that had come under the new Yugoslav state. In addition other refugees arrived from Thrace, which Greece had taken after the First World War. In the early 1930s, 11 per cent of Sofia's population consisted of post-1918 refugees from those two areas (not including children born to these refugees after their arrival in Bulgaria).

To Bulgarian eyes, the possibility of reopening the Macedonian issue via the idea of a Balkan Federation was attractive. For the Bulgarian Communist Party, which was much stronger and better organized than its Romanian counterpart, the idea represented good tactics. Unlike in Romania, there was a strong pro-Russian sentiment, particularly among the peasants and the less educated, dating back to Bulgaria's liberation by Russia from Ottoman role in the 1877–8 Russo-Turkish war.

For the communists in *Greece* next door, Macedonia was a big headache. The party's advocacy, in line with Comintern's policy, of an autonomous Macedonian state within a Balkan Federation undermined all its efforts to broaden its political influence among the Greek people.

11

Such a state would include the Greek portion of Macedonia, inhabited by almost 1.5m Greeks, of whom some 700,000 were refugees from Asia Minor, resettled after the 1921–2 Greek–Turkish war. The Greek communists' difficulties were compounded by the prospect that a future Balkan Federation would also involve autonomy for Greece's Western Thrace province: some of the Muslim population there regard themselves as Turks. The issue of Macedonia has continued to dog the Greek Left up to the present day.

In *Yugoslavia*, the picture was more complicated. The idea of the Yugoslav state's break-up into separate national units and their inclusion in a broader Balkan Federation held an obvious appeal for many of the country's non-Serbs, who saw the Yugoslav kingdom* – with its Serbian king (Alexander) and Serbian-dominated army and civil service – as Greater Serbia by another name.

It was precisely in Yugoslav *Macedonia* that the Balkan Federation project gained the communists strong political support. Officially designated as 'Southern Serbia' after 1918, Macedonia was exposed to systematic Serbianization. One of the features of this policy was the state-sponsored and heavily subsidized colonization by ethnic Serbs (including ex-soldiers) from other parts of Yugoslavia. The communists' popularity in Macedonia was reflected in the 1920 election for the Yugoslav Constituent Assembly: they got 38 per cent of the vote and emerged as the strongest party. (Later on, the communists lost much of this support, chiefly because of factional struggles in their own ranks among pro-Bulgarian, pro-Serb and outright Macedonian factions.)

In *Croatia*, too, where opposition to Serbian hegemony in the new state was strong, the communists achieved good electoral results before the party was banned in 1921. Later the Communist Party lost most of its original gains to the Croatian Peasant Party, which became the main channel for both national and social discontent among the Croats under its charismatic leader, Stjepan Radic.†

In *Slovenia*, the political scene was dominated by two 'bourgeois' parties, one liberal and one Catholic, and there was little antagonism to

---

* The unitary kingdom of Serbs, Croats and Slovenes, which came into being in December 1918, formally adopted the name Yugoslavia ('Yugo' meaning 'South') in October 1929.
† Radic died in August 1928, two months after being shot in the National Assembly in Belgrade by a Montenegrin deputy, Punisa Racic, who also murdered two other Croat deputies and wounded two others. In spite of this multiple murder, Racic got off lightly, with a sentence which he served in an open prison. It was only after 1945 that the communists sentenced him to death for collaboration with the Nazis during the Second World War and executed him.

Belgrade before 1941. The Communist Party was widely regarded as a fringe organization far removed from mainstream political activity. But the communists began to be taken more seriously when, in 1937, they set up a separate Slovene Communist Party within the Yugoslav Party (a parallel move was made in Croatia) and began to take up Slovene national concerns, such as the fear of German and Italian expansionism, within a broader anti-fascist framework. Neither the Slovene nor the Croat Party had any organizational independence, but the very fact of their existence made recruitment easier.

Within *Serbia*, communism benefited from the strong pro-Russian feelings that prevailed. As in Bulgaria, this was based on gratitude for backing in the past, not least in 1914, by the great Slav Orthodox power. It was reinforced by the Serbian habit of studying in Russia, and was relatively easily converted after 1917 into support for Soviet Russia among the younger generation.

But even those Serbs who – like the communists – were opposed to the monarchist regime never warmed to the idea of the break-up of the state and relished even less that of teaming up in a Balkan Federation with Serbia's next-door neighbour and bitter rival, Bulgaria. The Comintern line on Yugoslavia presented difficulties for those like Sima Markovic, Party Secretary in the 1920s, who – though personally indifferent to the nationality issue – were aware of its unpopularity among the Serbs. Markovic tried to cope with it by 'relativizing' nationality conflicts in Yugoslavia, portraying them as essentially a masked struggle over the distribution of wealth between the 'national bourgeoisies': the Serb one eager to overcome its own backwardness and wrest the dominant position in the country's economic and financial system from the more advanced capitalist Croat and Slovene bourgeoisies. These, in turn, according to this reading of the Yugoslav situation, were trying to force Serbia to stay a purely agrarian country. This intriguing and ingenious attempt to 'explain away' the nationality conflict in Yugoslavia failed to convince, not least because, for example, the bulk of the capital in Croatia and Slovenia was foreign.* In the mid-1930s, when the Comintern changed its line to support for an anti-fascist coalition of states, it no longer advocated the break-up of Yugoslavia. There was a broad welcome for the new line among the Serb Party members and sympathizers.

---

* An updated version of this theory was widely used by Serbian communist writers, with the same political aim of 'relativizing' the nationality question in Yugoslavia, in the 1970s and 1980s. They represented the current nationality conflicts in Yugoslavia as nothing more than 'turf fights' among the 'national politocracies' in individual republics.

A similar situation obtained in *Montenegro*, one of the Communist Party's strongest constituencies in Yugoslavia. There, as in Serbia, pro-Russian sentiment dated back to pre-1918 days when Montenegro, a tiny Christian Orthodox principality, received much political and material backing from Russia. This sentiment was later transferred to Soviet Russia.

The Kosovo conundrum

There were only a handful of Communist Party members before the Second World War among Yugoslavia's ethnic Albanians who, with the Macedonians, were the country's worst-treated national group. Concentrated in Kosovo and Western Macedonia, the Albanians were subjected by the Serbian authorities to systematic discrimination and various forms of pressure, including pressure to leave *en masse*. In 1940, a year after the signing of the Molotov–Ribbentrop Pact and the abandonment of the Popular Front line, the Yugoslav Party took a first step towards making it possible to recruit Kosovo Albanians: organizational autonomy was granted to the party committee for Kosovo, which had previously been under the regional party committee for Montenegro.

When in April 1941 Yugoslavia was invaded and dismembered by Germany and Italy, assisted by Bulgaria and Hungary, nowhere was the end of the Yugoslav state welcomed more warmly than among the Kosovo Albanians. And when, after the German attack on the Soviet Union in June 1941, Yugoslav communists began to organize guerrilla resistance, many local Serbs were ready to respond – but no ethnic Albanians. Participation in any struggle involving a return to Yugoslav (which, to the Albanians, meant Serbian) rule was anathema to the Albanians. 'Even the name "Yugoslavia" repels potential Party supporters', reported Svetozar Vukmanovic-Tempo, a senior Yugoslav Party official sent to the area to see what could be done.[5]

In Albania itself, there was no Communist Party proper before the Second World War, only some half a dozen groups of various ideological shades in the main towns. The most important of these turned out to be the one to which Enver Hoxha, the country's future ruler, belonged, in Korca in the south. The Communist Party of Albania (CPA), later renamed the Albanian Party of Labour, was formed, with help from the Communist Party of Yugoslavia (CPY), only in November 1941, after the Soviet Union had been invaded by Germany and the anti-fascist war provided a platform on which to unite. Enver Hoxha became its leader. The motivation of the CPY seems to have been that recruitment in

Kosovo could perhaps be facilitated if it established a subordinate, auxiliary Albanian Party.

Kosovo, portions of western Macedonia and an area on the eastern border of Montenegro had, meanwhile, been incorporated by the Axis powers into the new Greater Albania under Italian tutelage. The Italians provided food and arms and a measure of local autonomy. This removed from the Albanians any strong national motive for resistance. Nevertheless, resistance to the Italians did begin under the leadership of one or two chieftains. In 1942, Enver Hoxha and the fledgling CPA managed to join up with those chieftains to create the Movement of National Liberation (LNC). The communists seized the leadership of it from the start. Most of the country's chieftains and leaders stayed aloof, however. When they saw the leftist tendency of the LNC, they set up a rival and potentially stronger grouping called the Balli Kombetar (BK).

The Yugoslav Party criticized the CPA for having formed the LNC on too narrow a basis. In mid-1943, when it looked as if Italy was going to be knocked out of the war and Albania would be liberated, the Albanian communists responded to this criticism by trying to negotiate a common front between the LNC and the BK. An agreement was reached at Mukje in August 1943. It included a demand for self-determination in Kosovo – a *sine qua non* for every Albanian nationalist. But this was unacceptable to the Albanian Party's Yugoslav mentors, and Hoxha was forced to side with them and overturn the agreement, anathematizing the BK.

The rapid intervention of the Germans after the capitulation of Italy prevented the LNC from obtaining all the arms and equipment it needed for its newly forming partisan battalions. During the winter of 1943–4 successive German drives, actively or passively supported by the BK, wiped out the partisan units in the centre and north of Albania and nearly destroyed the new battalions in the south. But as spring approached, the destruction spread by the Germans and the BK stimulated recruitment for the partisans. They rapidly eclipsed the BK, gaining enough strength to muster a small army to strike back in the centre and the north.

One of the few chieftains who were founder-members of the LNC was Abas Kupi. After the Mukje fiasco, he broke away from the LNC and founded his own Zogist movement.[*] With the failure of the BK, he became the great hope for a 'nationalist' resistance in Albania; but the resistance never materialized. The British, insisting on resistance before supply, helped the LNC/partisans. Kupi, demanding supply, recognition

---

[*] Supporters of King Zog, who went into exile after Mussolini's invasion of Albania in 1939.

15

of King Zog and the promise of self-determination for Kosovo before resistance, had failed to meet British requirements before the partisans, in their northwards drive, overran his territory. The Albanian National Resistance Army (ANLA), led by Enver Hoxha, swept the board and set up a government which was completely in the hands of the CPA.

At this point, in the autumn of 1944, the intention of the CPY that the CPA should be a subordinate party began to cause friction. A new envoy from Tito intervened in the proceedings of the CPA's Politburo from October onwards and played an assertive part in the plenum of the novice CPA's Central Committee in November. He was critical of the CPA's (i.e., Hoxha's) line during the war. Hoxha, with the ANLA behind him, was too powerful in the moment of victory to be overthrown; but the Yugoslavs had the support of the second strong man in the CPA, Koci Xoxe, who had sided with them unhesitatingly at the time of the Mukje affair. The struggle for control of the party and hence of Albania continued until 1948. It was about to end in triumph for Xoxe and the Yugoslavs when Stalin's break with Tito unexpectedly handed victory to Hoxha.

Meanwhile, at the end of the war, Kosovo had become a contentious issue between the CPA and CPY. Already, towards the end of 1943, Vuk-manovic-Tempo had accused Enver Hoxha and his close colleague, Haxhi Lleshi, of overt Albanian chauvinism, which may explain why Hoxha was so quick to adopt the Yugoslav line at Mukje. In the autumn of 1944, the Yugoslavs had problems in 'liberating' Kosovo. The Albanians were brought in to make the task easier – in other words, Albanians would be 'liberated' by other Albanians. The ANLA sent two brigades into Kosovo in October 1944 and the force was raised to two divisions by the end of the year. The Yugoslavs contrived to move the Albanian forces out by the spring of 1945, and full Yugoslav control was then imposed on 'liberated' Kosovo, dashing any hopes on the part of the Kosovars of self-determination in favour of Albania. Enver Hoxha and his close supporters in Albania had to swallow the fact that they had been 'used' in this way by the CPY. It seems to have made them determined that, if Yugoslavia had Kosovo, it would not – if they could help it – have Albania as well.[6]

Yugoslavia's wartime agendas

In Yugoslavia, too, the Second World War was only partially the epic anti-fascist struggle that conventional history portrays. A closer look reveals a number of (often carefully concealed) national agendas. It could be argued that Tito owed his victory in 1944–5 above all to his understanding of these national concerns and to his skilful exploitation of them for his own non-nationalist power-seeking ends.

Tito certainly made mistakes but he also learnt from them. An example was his proclamation of a Soviet-style republic in western Serbia in the autumn of 1941. This failed to ignite the broader, all-Yugoslav revolution he was hoping for and made it easy for the Germans to eject the communists from there. National concerns predominated in Serbia at the time, ensuring that it remained out of the communists' reach until 1944, when the Red Army reached it from the east and liberated Belgrade, with the Yugoslav partisans' assistance. During the intervening period, Serbia stayed under the overall control of the Germans and the Vichy-style Serbian government of General Milan Nedic.

The third player in this complex relationship was General Draza Mihailovic, who started the first resistance to the Germans in May 1941 with a guerrilla force, popularly known as Cetniks, and was appointed Minister of War by the royalist Yugoslav government in exile in London. He negotiated with Tito about the possibility of uniting their efforts, but owing to the two leaders' completely different long-term aims (and hence proposed tactics), the attempt failed and they became the bitterest of enemies. After Tito's forces were expelled from Serbia by the Germans, Mihailovic ended up by operating what amounted to an informal understanding with the Nedic regime – justified by the need to preserve Serbia from the destruction likely to be inflicted on it by German reprisals for serious guerrilla resistance.

Mihailovic's strategy was based on the calculation that, as in the First World War, Serbia would be liberated by the victorious Western allies marching from the direction of Salonika or, perhaps, the Adriatic coast. This suited the Germans who, though opposed to Mihailovic, realized that the joint efforts of Nedic and Mihailovic successfully kept the communists out of Serbia. They were able to do so because the majority of the *Srbijanci*, Serbs from Serbia proper (*uza Srbija*),* decided that a policy of lying low was better suited to Serbia's national interests. At any rate, they felt it to be preferable to the communists' apparently reckless revolutionism, which many feared would lead to savage reprisals by the occupying forces and wholesale destruction of property.

Behind this lay the perception of many Serbs (and certainly of the Cetniks) that their most dangerous enemies in Yugoslavia were not actually the Germans, the Italians and their allies, the Bulgarians and the

---

* They are often differentiated from Serbs from 'over there' (*preko*), i.e. those west of the Drina and Danube rivers (in Croatia and Bosnia), who are called *Precani*.

Hungarians, but rather the other Yugoslavs, particularly the Croats (whether wearing partisan uniforms or those of the Croat quisling regime), the Bosnian Muslims and the Albanians. The so-called Ustasa ('insurgent') regime of Ante Pavelic first of all tried to expel the bulk of the Croat Serbs to German-occupied Serbia. When the Germans stopped further transports to Serbia because this was causing them political problems there, the Ustasas sent to concentration camps huge numbers of Serbs (together with Jews, Gypsies and anti-Pavelic Croats). Many thousands of Serbs (the exact figures are disputed) were killed in the wartime fascist Croat state; many others were expelled to Serbia proper.[7] This experience had a traumatic effect on Serbian consciousness and continued to form political perceptions afterwards. It is possible that a free and open debate among the peoples of Yugoslavia in the immediate aftermath of the Second World War about what actually happened between 1941 and 1945 – particularly about who did what to whom (including murders of Croats and Muslims by Serbian Cetniks) – could have dispelled some of the myths and moderated some of the hatreds generated by that period. However, the imposition of a heavily doctored communist version of events allowed the wartime hatreds to fester, feeding on the new grievances of the Tito era.

The Mihailovic movement's decision to adopt an essentially wait-and-see policy, combining collaboration with low-level resistance to the occupying forces by locally recruited Cetniks, had serious long-term consequences. Collaboration with the Italians and sometimes even the Germans – and, after 1942, the participation of Cetnik units in German and Italian operations against the Tito partisans – discredited the movement in the eyes of the British, whose main interest was short-term: the actual military struggle on the ground against the Axis powers. To this end they were ready to support whoever was prepared to kill the most Germans. This, of course, ruled out from the start those anti-communists in Slovenia, Croatia and Serbia itself who (whether out of conviction or purely tactically) had openly aligned themselves with the Axis powers. But it also sank the Cetniks, although the British reached the decision to stop backing them with the utmost reluctance and relatively late –towards the end of 1943. The loss of British support was a body blow to the Cetniks, politically as much as militarily. By the same token, British military and political backing was one of the key elements of the partisans' ultimate victory.

There were in fact three reasons why the British dropped Mihailovic in favour of Tito. In the first place, Tito had convinced them that, unlike Mihailovic, he was a serious military ally against the Germans. But he had also given a strong impression that, also unlike Mihailovic and his largely Serb Cetniks, he and his partisan movement enjoyed broad support among all the Yugoslav nations. Finally, his forces controlled a much larger 'liberated territory'.

As regards the first reason, there is a 'revisionist' school of thought which argues that the decision to switch from Mihailovic to Tito was a tragic mistake, due partly to over-optimistic reports by certain British liaison officers on Tito's military capabilities, partly to deliberate pro-Tito and anti-Mihailovic disinformation by communists and fellow-travellers in key British organizations such as the Special Operations Executive (SOE).[8]

The present vigorous debate about who was or was not really fighting the Germans and why, and about the communists' actual role in the British change of policy is still in full spate. More evidence is needed before any conclusive judgments can be reached. As far as Tito's military contribution is concerned, it does look as if it may have been over-estimated. The Germans never kept large formations in Yugoslavia (if one excludes those withdrawing from Greece and Albania in 1944 and early 1945). As for the Italians, it is true that in the summer of 1943 they had more than 300,000 troops stationed – or tied down, as some would have it – in Yugoslavia. But those Italian troops were there not primarily for military reasons – to fight the insurgents – but above all to provide visible back-up for Italy's position, conceded by Hitler, as a hegemonic power in the western Balkans.

As to the second question – which movement was more broadly based – it is incontrovertible that Mihailovic was politically hamstrung by his pan-Serb programme, which envisaged the purging of 'Serb lands' (including Bosnia and Hercegovina and large parts of Croatia) of non-Serbs. In contrast, Tito led a broad coalition made up of Serbs and non-Serbs alike. In addition to ideological anti-fascists from among all nationalities, this attracted:

(a) *Slovenes*, whose country was split between the Third Reich and Mussolini's Italy and whose survival, as a nation, was threatened in Hitler's 'new order'.
(b) *Serbs* from Croatia and Bosnia and Hercegovina, threatened with annihilation by the Ustasa regime. But not all of the Croat Serbs, fleeing from Pavelic's terror, ended up in Tito's partisan ranks. Some of them joined the Cetniks, especially in the Italian-occupied areas in the south, notably around Knin. The Italian authorities financed and

armed them as auxiliary forces to keep the partisans out but also to prevent the then Croat government from asserting its authority in Croat areas under Italian military occupation but not formally annexed by Italy.

(c) *Croats*, first from areas in the south annexed by Italy and then, from 1942 onwards, also elsewhere. The partisans' most important reservoir of recruitment consisted of Croats called up to serve in the regular Croat army – the so-called Domobrans (or 'defenders of the homeland') – who regularly handed themselves over to Tito in large numbers, together with their officers, weapons and equipment. The partisans were greatly helped by the Croats' reaction against Cetnik atrocities, particularly in southern Croatia and in Bosnia.

(d) *Bosnian Muslims*, wooed by Pavelic, who called them 'the flower of the Croat nation' and even built a mosque for them in Zagreb, Croatia's predominantly Catholic capital. Very soon, however, even the Muslims originally attracted by Pavelic started to cool off, disillusioned by the brutal nature of his regime. What attracted many of them to Tito was the promise of autonomy for Bosnia and Hercegovina and, as in the case of the Croats, the need for protection against the strongly anti-Muslim Cetniks.

(e) *Macedonians*, disillusioned with Bulgarian rule and attracted by Tito's promise of a Macedonian republic within a postwar Yugoslav federation.

(f) *Kosovo Albanians*, who had been talked with difficulty, very late on, into joining Tito by communists from Albania holding out the prospect of joining Albania proper.

Tito's nationality policy, though more successful than that of his domestic rivals, nevertheless came under strain within the party itself at certain times. There was, for example, considerable tension in the wake of Yugoslavia's dismemberment in 1941 between the central Yugoslav Party leadership, which was committed to the continuance of the Yugoslav state in some form, and the party organization in Macedonia under Metodi Satorov (whose conspiratorial party name was 'Sarlo'). Satorov accepted the new territorial arrangement under which the bulk of Macedonia was incorporated into Bulgaria, broke organizational links with the Yugoslav Party and incorporated his regional committee into the Bulgarian Communist Party. At first, Tito sought to discipline Satorov, but without success. The dispute was ostensibly about jurisdiction but actually it was both about future frontiers between Balkan states and about the best tactics to pursue in organizing an insurrection (Satorov had argued that he could not raise support in Macedonia within a Yugoslav framework, which would recall to his fellow-Macedonians the pre-1941 Serbianization policy).

The issue eventually went to the Comintern for adjudication. In line with Stalin's cautious policy of not wishing to challenge the validity of Allied countries' borders, the Comintern decided in favour of the Yugoslav Party, which expelled Satorov. However, when he went to Bulgaria, the Communist Party there welcomed him into its leadership.

Later on in the war, the partisan movement in Croatia achieved considerable success under the leadership of Andrija Hebrang, a senior party figure and an able and intelligent organizer. In 1943–4 it controlled a large and well-run 'liberated territory' in Croatia. But the movement came under suspicion of having become 'too Croat'. The specific charge investigated by, among others, Milovan Djilas was that it was too ready to cooperate with the non-communist Croat opposition to Pavelic and generally to make concessions to Croat national feeling.

Tito was particularly infuriated when the Croat partisan movement set up its own, Croat, news agency on 'liberated territory'. He was also incensed by the Croat partisans' decision in September 1943 to announce, quite independently and without reference to the central Yugoslav leadership, the reunification with Croatia of territories ceded to Italy by royalist Yugoslavia under the 1920 Treaty of Rapallo, and of others ceded by Pavelic's regime under the Venice Treaty of May 1941.

Hebrang argued that no other tactics were possible: one of the main criteria for success was sensitivity to the strong local national feeling. To no avail: after a high-level party investigation Hebrang was replaced by Vladimir Bakaric, a more junior and pliable man, dispatched to the just-liberated Belgrade in October 1944 and given a series of economic posts, without a strong power base. Hebrang was arrested in 1948, accused of siding with Stalin, and subsequently died in mysterious circumstances in prison, allegedly by committing suicide.[*]

---

[*] Later, the Yugoslav authorities produced documents purporting to show that Hebrang, who had been captured by the Pavelic police early in the war and subsequently exchanged for some high-ranking officials held by the partisans, had become a Pavelic spy 'turned' while in prison. New evidence brought to Zagreb from Belgrade in 1985 appears to confirm what had long been suspected: that the spying charge was a clumsy fabrication designed to blacken Hebrang's reputation posthumously. It also appears to confirm the widespread suspicion that he was murdered in prison. The non-communist Croat government elected in May 1990 has ordered a judicial investigation of the whole Hebrang case, which is still continuing.

21

Map 3 The Balkans in 1945

© Vladimir Pavlinic, 1991

Paths to power

Not surprisingly, it took a good deal of Soviet effort to establish communist rule in Romania, where communism had been a marginal political force. The process was easier in Bulgaria, where there had been some wartime communist guerrilla resistance, but in both countries communist rule had clearly been imposed from outside. It was easier in Albania and Yugoslavia, where the local communists had managed to mobilize considerable support. The difference, crucial in an area such as the Balkans, was between those who had come to power by working with the grain of national feeling, as Tito had done in Yugoslavia and Hoxha in Albania, and those like the Bulgarian and Romanian communists, who owed their power totally to an external agency, Moscow.

Romania

Of the four regimes, the Romanian was the weakest and therefore the most dependent on Moscow's backing. However, there were two factors that helped Romanian communists to consolidate their power. First, because the country had not experienced either civil war or physical devastation as a result of wartime operations on its territory, the whole of the state apparatus was in place and, after purges in the army and the civil service, ready to serve the new masters. Second, the non-communists still feared in the immediate post-1945 period that, since Romania was a former enemy country, the Western Allies might prevent it from regaining northern Transylvania (which had been awarded by the Axis powers to Hungary in 1940). Soviet support was, therefore, seen as essential in securing this vital national objective and the communists, as Moscow's friends, were best placed to secure it. This tactic proved correct. Romania managed, with Stalin's backing, to get northern Transylvania back. This was a strong boost for the communists.

Bulgaria

The Bulgarian Communist Party was larger than the Romanian one. In September 1944, it claimed to have some 25,000 members. Non-communists asserted that the real figure was more like 8,000 – but this was still eight times more than Romania. The Bulgarian Party, like its Romanian counterpart, was helped in the immediate postwar period by two factors. First, the non-communists believed that the closeness of party members to Moscow (notably that of people like Georgi Dimitrov, a senior Comintern figure) could help prevent the imposition on Bulgaria of heavy wartime reparations like those that had crippled its economy after the First World War. This feeling was so strong that the opposition held back for patriotic reasons. Second, the communists were able to play on the Bulgarians' psychological need, understandable in a nation that had been repeatedly defeated in wars this century, for a powerful shield against a hostile world – the Soviet Union.

None of this, however, resulted in milder, more tolerant communist policies towards the Bulgarian opposition. Most prominent members of the non-communist parties were 'liquidated' within six months of the Soviet army's entry into Bulgaria in September 1944. The Bulgarian authorities instituted a purge which, per head of population, claimed more victims than in any other East European country. By March 1945, the 'people's courts' had tried 11,667 people and, of those, 2,138 were sentenced to death. Unofficial estimates put the number of victims at between 30,000 and 100,000.[9] The Bulgarian army, the strongest and best organized force that could have opposed the communists, was sent to fight alongside the Soviet army against the Germans in Hungary and Austria. By the time it came back, the communists held all the main levers of power. The army was thoroughly purged and provided with Soviet-style political commissars.

Albania
The Albanian communists, in contrast, approached power in November 1944 in a mood of self-confidence based on the (not entirely unjustified) feeling that they had freed the country from foreign forces and defeated their domestic rivals largely by their own efforts. That self-confidence was shaken somewhat by the emergence of the Kosovo problem as a bone of contention with the powerful Yugoslav Communist Party. At the meeting of the Albanian Central Committee in November 1944, just before the communists' entry into Tirana, the capital, a Yugoslav representative attending the meeting shocked many Albanian communists by suggesting that Albania and Yugoslavia be joined in one state. The incident revealed a division within Albanian ranks, with Enver Hoxha opposed and Koci Xoxe, a powerful party figure, in favour. The plan was neither accepted nor rejected: it stayed on the agenda. The Hoxha group argued for an independent foreign policy based on friendly relations with East and West alike and, in domestic affairs, a policy of postponing radical socialist measures until agriculture and industry had advanced within the framework of a market economy. The Xoxe group pressed for immediate union and, in domestic policy, a full-blooded Bolshevik pro-

gramme of social transformation similar to that embarked upon by the Yugoslav communists. This debate, resolved at first under Yugoslav pressure in the Xoxe group's favour, gave a foretaste of the full-scale conflict between Yugoslavia and Albania after 1948.

Yugoslavia

The Yugoslav communists displayed an even greater self-confidence when they attained power in the whole of Yugoslavia in the spring of 1945. In this euphoric mood, they ignored Soviet warnings to behave more circumspectly so as not to embarrass the Soviet Union in its relations with the Western Allies. Their cockiness was reflected in equal measure in their domestic and foreign policies. At home, the Tito regime launched an ambitious industrialization programme preceded by the fastest and most sweeping nationalization anywhere in Eastern Europe. Tito's foreign policy was even more spectacular. He challenged the Western Allies, unsuccessfully as it happened, in Austria and Trieste. In the south, Yugoslavia was the chief backer of the communist side in the Greek civil war. Tito and the Bulgarian Party leader, Georgi Dimitrov, had a plan for a South-East European Union. Behind all this lay Tito's long-term aim, clearly understood by Stalin, to form a South-East European grouping under his leadership. Stalin's realization that Tito could become a serious threat to his own hegemony in Eastern Europe was the main reason for Tito's expulsion from the Soviet bloc in 1948 after he refused to toe the line.

Tito's confidence rested to a large degree on his knowledge that his own aims were broadly in harmony with the national aims of the peoples of Yugoslavia. What these aims offered them above all was protection against traditional enemies: the Slovenes from Italy and Germany; the Croats from Italy and, even more important, from Serbia; and the Macedonians from Greece and Serbia but also from Bulgaria. What they offered the Serbs, however, was less than the total and undisputed dominance they had enjoyed in the prewar kingdom. Herein lay the seeds of the Serb backlash that followed the Tito era.

In Tito's Yugoslavia, the Serbs got a republic consisting of Serbia proper with the nominally autonomous provinces of Vojvodina in the north and, most important, Kosovo, centre of Serbia's medieval state, in the south. In addition, during the first two postwar decades, the Serbs enjoyed a dominant position in Croatia and Bosnia, despite being a minority of the population there. This dominance lasted right up to the dismissal in 1966 of Aleksandar Rankovic, a Serb and the powerful

25

security chief and party cadre secretary; it was due to the large preponderance of Serbs in the party, the army and the security services in those two republics. This stemmed from their massive participation in the partisan ranks in Croatia as a result of their persecution by the Pavelić regime. Many Cetniks joined the partisans after an amnesty in 1943. Tito's mobilization in Serbia in 1944 for the expulsion of the Germans and the final victory, which he wanted to achieve without Russian help, also increased the proportion of Serbs in the army.

From the party's point of view, there was something to be said for soothing the Serbs' feelings over what many of them regarded as two bitter losses. The first was that Bosnia, a key element in Serbia's national expansion programme since the middle of the nineteenth century, had not been formally joined with Serbia under the new federal arrangement, despite strenuous efforts by some Serbian communists. The Serbs regarded their informal control in Bosnia in the first two postwar decades as necessarily impermanent. This was a correct calculation, as was proved when the more numerous Muslims subsequently became the dominant group there at the end of the 1960s.

The other loss, from the point of view of the Serbian national agenda, was the 'abandonment' of Macedonia ('Old Serbia' in prewar Yugoslavia) through the granting of federal autonomy to the Macedonian Republic. This meant in effect the abandonment of landlocked Serbia's *Drang nach Saloniki*, its plan to gain access to the Aegean Sea.[*]

The other three communist regimes in the Balkans – the Albanian one divided and the Bulgarian and Romanian ones lacking in self-confidence – were not able to draw upon as wide a national consensus as the Tito regime. They were obliged to recognize Yugoslavia's clear regional supremacy, though not for long.

---

[*] The Germans played on this Serbian ambition when, in negotiations in early 1941 designed to induce the then royal Yugoslav government to join the Tripartite Pact (Germany, Italy and Japan), they promised it Greek Macedonia with the port of Salonika. This promise was recorded in a secret protocol that accompanied Yugoslavia's adherence to the Pact on 25 March 1941. The Axis connection was repudiated in a British-inspired officers' coup two days later. This brought Yugoslavia warm praise from Winston Churchill but also provoked Hitler's rage and led to Yugoslavia's annihilation at the hands of the Wehrmacht the following month.

Chapter 3

The Cold War corset

For much of the period between the two world wars, the Great Powers displayed a policy of benign neglect towards the Balkans: the United States because of the onset of isolationism after 1919; Britain and France because they were engaged elsewhere; and the Soviet Union and Germany because they were temporarily disabled – the former by revolution and civil war, the latter by military defeat. The only European power to pursue an active policy in the area was Italy, one of the victors in 1918 but not particularly happy with its territorial gains. Against the pro-French Little Entente (Czechoslovakia, Romania and Yugoslavia), which was designed to maintain the status quo, Italy backed the anti-Versailles, 'revisionist' regimes in Austria, Bulgaria and Hungary and supported Croat groups working for Yugoslavia's disintegration (notably the Pavelic Ustasa group). This support lasted until well into the 1930s, when Italy reached an understanding with Belgrade.

The Balkans assumed greater strategic importance in the mid-1930s with the re-emergence of Germany as a serious competitor to Italy; the Soviet Union continued to operate chiefly through the local communist parties. The outbreak of war and subsequent events, including the communist takeover in Albania, Bulgaria, Romania and Yugoslavia, described in Chapter 2, accelerated the process. Soon the region had regained its pre-1914 status as an important theatre of Great Power conflict. The Western allies conceded the Soviet Union's predominance in Bulgaria and Romania, exactly as had been foreshadowed in the informal 'percentages' understanding over the division of spheres of interest reached by Churchill and Stalin in Moscow in October 1944.[10] They lost out in Yugoslavia, where there should have been a 50:50 relationship, and in Albania, over which there had been no agreement. But the Western powers could – and did – hold their ground in Greece and Turkey. First Britain helped the non-communist Greek government defeat a communist attempt to seize power in 1944–5. Then in 1947–8, in order to contain the Soviet threat in south-eastern Europe and the Mediterranean, the United States offered military and economic assistance to both Greece and Turkey. This culminated in their membership of Nato. A major role was played in the defeat of the Greek communists after 1945 by Tito's decision after his expulsion from Cominform (the Communist Information Bureau) in 1948 to reduce his support for the Greek guerrillas and then in July 1949 to close the frontiers of Yugoslavia to them.

Yugoslavia's expulsion from the Soviet bloc threatened to destabilize the post-1945 Balkan alignment. But the brief period of uncertainty ended relatively quickly when the Western powers stepped in, providing Yugoslavia with military and economic aid and even a link with Nato through the Balkan Pact between Greece, Turkey and Yugoslavia, signed in February 1953. This more or less restored the 50:50 ratio, although the fact that Yugoslavia remained communist under Tito's leadership represented an important guarantee in Moscow's eyes. The stand-off over Yugoslavia between the West and the Soviet Union remained in force for more than three decades, even beyond Tito's death in 1980.

Albania's balancing act

After the communists had taken over in Albania, the country was rapidly turned into a satellite of Yugoslavia, which in its turn was then still a satellite (though, admittedly, already an awkward one) of the Soviet Union. Albania's dependent position was reflected in the treaty of friendship, cooperation and mutual aid it signed with Yugoslavia in July 1946. The treaty envisaged the coordination of economic plans between the two countries, the standardization of their monetary systems, the creation of a customs union and the unification of prices. To implement these policies, a large number of Yugoslav experts were sent to Albania and given key positions in government departments and the armed forces. Serbian was made a compulsory subject in Albanian schools. Joint-stock companies were set up to exploit Albania's oil and other minerals. The Albanians much resented their own unequal status, as junior partners, in these companies. (Ironically, one of the reasons for the growing resentment of the Soviet Union among Yugoslavia's own leaders was Moscow's imposition of similar bodies on them at about the same time.) Like Italy before it, Yugoslavia supplied half of Albania's budget needs.

In reality, Albania had become a vassal state on the road to full absorption into what most Albanians saw as another version of Serbia. Keeping it in that position was the job of the pro-Yugoslav faction in the leadership. This was led by Koci Xoxe, who took on the mantle of Esad Pasha, the vassal of the prewar, royalist Yugoslavia. Though a minority, the Xoxe faction, with the help of the numerous Yugoslav personnel in Albania, ensured compliance with Belgrade's wishes. Some opponents of union with Yugoslavia were purged. Nako Spiru, who was in charge of economic policy in Albania, found himself caught in an insoluble conflict of interests and committed suicide in November 1947. Mehmet Shehu, Xoxha's military strong man, was pushed out of office shortly afterwards, although he reappeared after the break with Yugoslavia in 1948.

The Tito–Stalin dispute was a godsend to Hoxha and his faction. His own survival was due to a combination of cunning and a willingness to eat humble pie – which he could afford to do when appropriate because of his dominant position within the party's and the army's wartime cadres. Hoxha and his supporters were jubilant when Yugoslavia was expelled from Cominform. This had been set up in 1947, with its headquarters in Belgrade, and was supposed to act as a replacement in Europe for the Comintern, which had been disbanded in 1943 in order to reassure the Western Allies that the Soviet Union would not use the war to promote the cause of world revolution.

Albania immediately repudiated all its economic agreements with Yugoslavia on the grounds that they were incompatible with national sovereignty, and expelled all Yugoslav civilian and military advisers and other personnel. Albania became the first East European state to line up behind the Soviet Union in its campaign against Yugoslavia – a move which not only reflected the Albanian regime's hostility towards Belgrade but also its sense of insecurity from the continuing Anglo-American attempts to overthrow it. A few months later, the Soviet Union concluded an agreement with Albania under which it promised to make good the economic and technical aid Albania had forfeited because of its break with Yugoslavia.

It is easy to understand the Albanian leaders' elation. First, Yugoslavia's disgrace had, at one and the same time, removed the danger of Albania's absorption by its bigger neighbour and given it what it had always wanted: a distant patron which had no territorial designs on it and yet was willing to protect it against not only Yugoslavia but also Greece and its Western allies – as well as giving it economic aid. Second, the Soviet–Yugoslav conflict raised Albanian hopes, later to be disappointed, that

Yugoslavia might have to disgorge its Albanians and thus make possible the union of all Albanians in one state under communist leadership. Last but not least, the dispute provided Enver Hoxha with an opportunity to get rid of Koci Xoxe and other pro-Yugoslav leaders. In May 1949 Xoxe was tried in Tirana for high treason and sentenced to death.

Albania did well out of the Soviet–Yugoslav dispute. By hitching itself directly to the bigger ship, it obtained significant financial help (estimated at $600 million) from the Soviet Union for numerous projects. These included a number of hydroelectric power stations, which made an important contribution to Albania's energy supply. The Soviet naval presence in a submarine base in Vlore across the southern Adriatic from Italy was a mark of the strategic importance attached to small Albania by its distant but powerful ally.

But the Soviet–Albanian honeymoon did not survive Stalin. The Soviet–Yugoslav rapprochement, which began in 1954 and culminated in Nikita Khrushchev's visit to Belgrade in 1955 and Tito's to Moscow in 1956, was a dangerous time for Enver Hoxha. He feared, not without reason, that he and his country might be sacrificed by Khrushchev in the interests of good relations with Tito. Khrushchev wanted to harness Tito's influence in Eastern Europe for his own ends. Once more the Albanians had a last-minute escape, thanks to the outbreak of a new quarrel between Belgrade and Moscow in 1957. But they remained on their guard. Indeed, in 1960 it looked as if, yet again, Albania might be quietly abandoned by Moscow as part of a new Soviet–Yugoslav rapprochement – until the Sino-Soviet dispute presented the Albanians with a lifeline, and a new distant patron.

In the course of 1961, Soviet submarines were withdrawn from the naval base at Vlore, and Soviet and East European credits promised for 1961–5 were cancelled. China promptly stepped in and announced that it was giving Albania $125 million worth of credits – roughly what the Soviet bloc would have offered. Chinese specialists replaced those withdrawn from Albania by the Soviet Union and other East European countries. For Albania, the cost of the switch was great in material terms – its five-year plan had been geared to deliveries from the Soviet Union and Eastern Europe – but the alliance with China, the most populous country in the world, was an important boost to the Albanian regime's prestige. It was further enhanced when the Sino-Soviet dispute later erupted into a full-scale ideological conflict and small Albania became, with China, the Mecca of pure Marxist-Leninists from all over the world.

Romania's bid for independence

The Sino-Soviet split also helped the Romanian communist regime to broaden its originally extremely narrow base of support in the country by demonstrating to the population that it was ready and able to stand up to the Soviet Union in defence of Romania's national interests. In the immediate postwar period Romania was, of all the East European countries, the most exploited by the Soviet Union. Moscow imposed heavy reparations, classifying it, along with Bulgaria and Hungary, as a former enemy country. Romania's switch to the Allied side in August 1944 did not help in this respect. Merchant ships and railway rolling stock were impounded and transported to the Soviet Union, as were large quantities of industrial and semi-manufactured goods. Even whole plants were dismantled and removed. The Soviet–Romanian joint-stock companies controlled all sectors of economic life, including crude oil, uranium, chemicals, timber and shipping. German assets seized by the Soviet authorities provided Soviet capital. Romanian exports to and imports from the Soviet Union suffered from price discrimination.

Even later on, in the second half of the 1950s and the early 1960s, when the Soviet Union started to shore up the troubled East European economies, Romania remained bottom of the list – despite the fact that it was a key supplier to the Soviet economy of oil products, uranium, timber and foodstuffs. The gap between Romania and the more advanced East European countries widened, with the prospect – at that time perceived as intolerable by the country's communists and non-communists alike – that Romania would remain the lowly supplier of food and raw materials to the industrialized parts of the Soviet bloc. The tight Soviet grip on the Romanian economy reinforced the already strong anti-Soviet feeling among the population. More important, the knowledge that Romania was being discriminated against in comparison with the other East European countries caused intense frustration to many in the Romanian *nomenklatura*.

Stalin's death left Romania's hardline and deeply unpopular leadership in an exposed position. Its sense of vulnerability increased with the onset of the de-Stalinization campaign in the Soviet bloc in the wake of Khrushchev's speech denouncing Stalin in February 1956. Two other events in the autumn of 1956 made the Romanian leaders increasingly nervous: the political upheaval in Poland and, even more, the outbreak of the Hungarian revolution, with its political echoes among the Hungarian population in Transylvania. The withdrawal in 1958 of Soviet troops, which had been stationed in Romania since 1944, provoked further

31

reappraisal. Though unpopular with the people as a symbol of Soviet dominance, these troops had represented to the Romanian regime – as they had to others in Eastern Europe – an important political guarantee. Something else was needed to replace it. The time had come to play the nationalist card.

It was no accident that Romania started to play that card when it did – in 1960–61. The time was right. First of all, the Sino-Soviet split gave the Romanian leadership unexpected room for manoeuvre, just as it did the Albanians. At that moment, anybody opposing Moscow in the Soviet bloc was exceptionally safe. For Moscow, disciplining recalcitrant satellites like Romania would have meant diverting attention and energy from the far more urgent task of responding to China's difficult challenge.

Secondly, the ruling group was united behind the party leader, Gheorge Gheorghiu-Dej, a 'home communist' who had spent the 1933–44 period in Romanian gaols. It had an attractive cause – Romania's modernization and industrialization – that appealed both to the party elite and to the ordinary people. Gheorghiu-Dej and his colleagues, notably Nicolae Ceausescu, who was to succeed him on his death in 1965, simply broadened this into a direct appeal to Romanian nationalism in every other sphere. They were quite consciously playing on feelings which some of them had in any case quietly shared with their fellow-Romanians, above all the view of Romania as a rather superior island of Latinity surrounded by a Slav sea.

That is why the new, more openly nationalist policy had a strong cultural content. Quite apart from separating the Romanians neatly from the Slavs and the Hungarians, more immediate tactical benefits could be gained from the renewed publicity and emphasis given to Romanian national history. It was obviously politically useful to the regime, in a country where aversion to Russia ran deep, to be able to draw parallels between the resistance to the Romans of the Dacians (from whom modern Romanians claim descent) and contemporary resistance to Soviet domination. Invariably, the Romanian public responded patriotically, which was extremely gratifying to the regime.

Although the stress in the 1960s and the 1970s may have been on anti-Russianism, it was kept within very careful limits. This was to avoid a head-on challenge to Moscow on any important issue, not least over Bessarabia, which had become the Moldavian Soviet Republic after 1945. The Romanian regime never once formally raised the issue with Moscow until Ceausescu's downfall in December 1989. Even when, under Mikhail Gorbachev, public unrest in Moldavia came out into the open, with demands for help from Romania, the Ceausescu regime studiously ignored such demands.

From Moscow's point of view, an independent Romanian foreign policy was actually never considered a serious threat. Surrounded by communist states, Romania was in no position – even if it wanted to – to declare itself neutral, let alone switch alliances. As for establishing a multi-party political system, Moscow knew very well that that was the last thing Romania's Stalinist leadership was interested in. In fact, it relied on the Soviet connection as the ultimate guarantee of its own domestic monopoly of power. But for all that, Moscow was not prepared simply to tolerate certain Romanian foreign policy initiatives and wanted to warn the country's leaders not to overstep the limit.

A conduit was to hand for conveying such warnings: Hungary, a faithful follower of the Soviet foreign policy line ever since the communists took full power there in 1948.* The chosen method of warning Romania off was Soviet-approved Hungarian criticism of Romania's nationality policy. One warning came in the wake of the Soviet-led Warsaw Pact invasion of Czechoslovakia in August 1968, which Romania had refused to take part in and publicly condemned. Another warning was issued in June 1971 when the Soviet leadership was worried by the possibility that China might be in the process of establishing a sphere of influence in the Balkans. A senior Hungarian Politburo member referred publicly to the position of the Hungarian minority in Romania as a cause of difficulties in relations between the two countries.

By way of response, Romanian historians, with plenty of official encouragement, stepped up their efforts to prove that Transylvania had, ever since Roman times, been under continuous occupation, first by the Dacians, then by their direct descendants. The Hungarians' argument was that, on the contrary, during the Dark Ages and Early Middle Ages Transylvania had become 'empty' – to be settled later by the Hungarians, the Germans and, of course, also the Romanians, staying under (direct or indirect) Hungarian rule until 1918. The Romanian defensiveness was not based on a fear that Hungary, a country half Romania's size, could realistically hope to take Transylvania back by its own efforts. For the status quo to be altered in its favour, Hungary would need a powerful ally or allies, as it did in 1940 when it acquired northern Transylvania with backing from Hitler and Mussolini. In postwar Eastern Europe, this ally

---

* There was, of course, a brief exception between October and early November 1956 under the multi-party government of Imre Nagy, which was swiftly overthrown by direct Soviet military intervention.

could only be the Soviet Union. But Moscow, mindful of the need to avoid bringing into question Soviet post-1945 territorial conquests, carefully refrained from doing anything that could, however indirectly, upset the territorial status quo in Eastern Europe. Clearly, though, this did not stop the Soviet leaders making tactical use of temporarily dormant territorial disputes as a means of putting pressure on their smaller allies.

With increasing liberalization in Hungary, the issue of Transylvania began to slip out of the control of the authorities in Budapest and was gradually taken over in the late 1970s and the early 1980s by the opposition movement. Espousing the cause of the Hungarians in Transylvania was useful to the opposition because it broadened its base of support, by combining the inevitably less popular concern for human rights and civil liberties with a far wider patriotic appeal.

These developments worried the Ceausescu regime, whose prestige abroad was harmed by the unfavourable international attention being drawn to its repression of the Hungarian minority at home. It was perhaps even more urgently concerned about the effect the renewed public Hungarian interest in Transylvania might have on Romania's Hungarians. It responded by deliberately fostering an old-style chauvinism, with a particularly strong anti-Hungarian edge to it, through various government-supported organizations.*

Bulgaria's uneasy course

The regime in Bulgaria, as in Albania, had to swallow a bitter pill in the immediate aftermath of the Second World War. Putting up with the position of junior partner *vis-à-vis* the Tito regime in Yugoslavia was particularly galling for Bulgarian communists because of their party's longer revolutionary pedigree and the fact that it was headed by one of the most senior figures of the world communist movement. Georgi Dimitrov had achieved world-wide fame in 1934 by his defiance at the trial staged by the Nazis in order to implicate the communists in the fire that had destroyed the Reichstag building in Berlin shortly after Hitler came to power. Nevertheless, Bulgaria's communist partisans never numbered more than 10,000 to 15,000, whereas Tito enjoyed the glam-

---

*Even after the downfall of the Ceausescu regime in 1989, the tactic was still used. In the immediate aftermath of Ceausescu's fall, a body called Vatra Romaneasca (Romanian Hearth) was established with help from certain old party strata. It was dedicated to the 'patriotic education' of the Romanian masses, and has continued to play a prominent role in spreading anti-Hungarian propaganda among the population.

our of a successful revolutionary leader whose partisan movement could boast of having achieved power by its own efforts.

The Macedonian muddle

Bulgaria's junior position involved, above all, accepting the incorporation of Macedonia into Yugoslavia as one of its federal republics. In the nineteenth century, there was widespread agreement among European scholars that the Slav inhabitants of Macedonia were Bulgarians. However, the Serbs, who had achieved autonomy from the Ottoman empire in 1829 and who had plans to expand their territory southwards, westwards and northwards, claimed Macedonia right down to Salonika on ethnic grounds, asserting that its Slav inhabitants were Serbs. The Greeks, who had achieved their independence in 1832 and who had plans to expand northwards, based their claim to Macedonia on both historical and ethnic grounds. The Treaty of San Stefano in 1878, concluded at the end of the Russo-Turkish war, had given the newly independent Bulgaria the whole of Macedonia. But later that year it was returned to Turkey, following the nullification of the treaty at the Berlin Congress. This was at the joint insistence of Britain and Austria-Hungary, neither of which was willing to contemplate a new state beholden to Russia reaching as far as the Aegean. Restoration of the San Stefano borders became Bulgaria's national goal.

Rivalry between Bulgaria, Greece and Serbia over Macedonia, a Balkan 'no man's land' – accompanied by fighting among armed irregulars of all nationalities – remained one of the central issues of Balkan politics for the following two decades. In 1912 the three Christian Balkan countries decided to sink their differences. Together with tiny Montenegro, they formed the Balkan League, which immediately declared war on Turkey, hoping to benefit from its involvement in a war with Italy. Turkey was overwhelmingly defeated. The victors fell out over the division of the spoils and a new war broke out, with Bulgaria on one side and Greece, Montenegro, Romania and Serbia on the other. Bulgaria lost and sought to avenge itself by siding with the Central Powers during the First World War. Having found itself on the losing side, Bulgaria ended with only the small region of Pirin Macedonia. The bulk of Macedonia was divided between Greece and the new Yugoslavia, Serbia's successor-state.

Bulgaria's brief period of triumph in the Second World War included the recapture of Yugoslav Macedonia and, in 1941, the occupation of Thrace in Greece. But in 1944 Bulgaria was obliged to give back the portion of Macedonia it had taken away from Yugoslavia, once again retaining only Pirin Macedonia. In addition it was forced to give back to

35

Greece not only Thrace but also Greek Macedonia, which the Germans had allowed it to occupy as well. Bulgaria's brutal occupation of Thrace left behind a legacy of bitterness.

In 1944, Bulgarian and Yugoslav communists agreed to recognize the existence of a separate Macedonian nationality. They did so, however, with completely opposite motives. The Tito regime, whose foreign policy goals were nothing if not ambitious, saw the recognition of Macedonian nationality as a step towards the eventual unification of all Macedonians, including those in Bulgaria and Greece, under Yugoslav leadership. In the shorter term, the Tito regime hoped that the Macedonians' recognition as a nation on a par with the Serbs, the Croats and other fully-fledged Yugoslav nations would help to bind them more closely to Yugoslavia, from which they had been alienated by the pre-1941 Serbianization policy. By the same token, Belgrade hoped that the recognition of a separate Macedonian nationality would also undermine Bulgaria's claim, as well as loosening still further Macedonia's connection with Bulgaria. This had already been weakened by the indifferent treatment it had received under Bulgarian rule from 1941 to 1944.

For their part, the Bulgarian communists realized that in the wake of defeat Bulgaria was in no position to renew and actively pursue its claim on Macedonia. On the other hand, they hoped that the recognition of a separate Macedonian nationality would, for the time being at any rate, serve as an obstacle to further assimilation by the Greeks and the Serbs. The unspoken hope here was that Macedonia, because of its historical and ethnic links, would continue to gravitate towards Bulgaria and, in the fullness of time, perhaps even reunite with it formally. Since a Macedonian Republic could achieve unification with Bulgaria more easily within a common framework that included Yugoslavia in a Balkan Federation, the Bulgarian communists were in favour of the Federation when it was revived in 1944. From 1944 to 1948 the Bulgarian Communist Party even officially supported the idea of the secession of Pirin Macedonia to a Macedonian Socialist Federal Republic within the future Balkan Federation. However, in 1948 Stalin vetoed the project for such a federation.

Yugoslavia's expulsion from the Cominform in June 1948 came as a relief to Bulgaria. It released it from the embarrassing commitment to give up Bulgarian territory. The Bulgarian regime continued to recognize the Macedonian nationality, not least in order to keep its own Macedonians loyal in the political and propaganda conflict with Yugoslavia. But links with Yugoslav Macedonia were severed. After the death in July 1949 of Georgi Dimitrov, who had strong links with Macedonia (both his parents came from there), the policy began to change. First, the regime declared that the process of forming a separate Macedonian nationality had begun only in 1918. Later the date was moved to 1944. In April 1956, the Bulgarian Party decided at a plenary meeting of its Central Committee to withdraw its recognition of the existence of a separate Macedonian nationality. This was done as a concession to rising Bulgarian nationalism. Despite this important change in policy, the next census, held in December 1956, still provided an entry for a separate Macedonian nationality and showed that there were 187,789 'Macedonians' in Bulgaria. It was only in 1960 that the official Bulgarian statistical yearbook ceased to show a separate entry for the Macedonians. The first renewed Bulgarian claims to Macedonia appeared in a discreet form in 1958 in connection with the eightieth anniversary of the San Stefano Treaty. But the Bulgarian claims always carefully referred to Macedonia's 'Bulgarian past', coupled with statements affirming the political status quo.

Yugoslavia responded very promptly the same year, setting up, under its own Metropolitan, a separate Macedonian Orthodox church. This was indeed unusual – an atheist communist regime actually helping to set up a church – but it was not unprecedented. After all, in 1943 Stalin had reconstituted the virtually extinct Russian Orthodox hierarchy his regime had all but destroyed, because he badly needed the bishops to call on the Russian masses to fight for 'holy Russia'. The people had already shown, by surrendering *en masse* to the Germans in the early days of the war, that they were reluctant to die for Stalin and communism. Yugoslavia had made a shrewd political move with regard to the Macedonian church. In an Orthodox setting, an autocephalous church is one of the highest attributes of nationhood. To soothe Serb feelings (the Macedonian Orthodox had, ever since Serbia acquired Macedonia in 1913, been under the jurisdiction of the Serbian Patriarch), the newly established church decided to remain in canonical unity with the Serbian Orthodox church.

With these moves Yugoslavia consolidated its hold on Macedonia. Particularly upsetting for Bulgaria was the Soviet Union's apparent acquiescence, which turned into something even worse from the Bulgarian point of view. In 1962, Patriarch Alexis of Moscow, head of the Russian Orthodox church, visited Skopje, the capital of the Yugoslav Republic of Macedonia, and met the Macedonian Archbishop. In view of the close control exercised over the Russian Orthodox church by the Soviet authorities, there could hardly have been a clearer way of demonstrating Soviet recognition of the Macedonian nationality. In 1967, the

Macedonian Archbishop was upgraded to Patriarch. The outraged Serbian Orthodox bishops wanted to anathematize not only the Macedonians concerned but also all Yugoslav officials who had a hand in the matter. A head-on and politically damaging clash with Serbian nationalism, which the Serbian Orthodox church embodied, was narrowly averted by pressure on the Serbian Patriarch, a pliable man close to the authorities.

The patriotic campaign

As long as the Soviet–Yugoslav rapprochement continued, Bulgaria had to behave circumspectly over national questions. Its moment came with the invasion of Czechoslovakia in 1968, to which Bulgaria made a token contribution but which Yugoslavia condemned. This enabled the regime to expand the propaganda campaign that had begun in a low key in 1967 and that aimed to identify the party with Bulgarian patriotism. The campaign had followed an abortive coup in April 1965, led by a group of nationalist-minded senior Bulgarian army officers unhappy with the regime's humiliating subservience to Moscow, which had demonstrated the weakness of the party and its leader, Todor Zhivkov. The Bulgarian regime lost much support after turning away from economic reform in 1968. Its unpopularity increased in the 1970s as economic growth failed to produce any political relaxation and Zhivkov continued to pursue a slavishly pro-Soviet line.

Meanwhile, Bulgaria's image abroad continued to be blackened by a series of scandals like the 'poisoned umbrella tip' case in 1978, involving the murder in London of the well-known Bulgarian dissident, Georgi Markov, by an unknown assailant suspected of being a Bulgarian agent; and the assassination attempt on Pope John II, also widely attributed to Bulgaria's secret service. The regime was also worried about its unpopularity with the young, among whom the appeal of Western culture and ideas was growing. The culmination of the 'patriotic' campaign was reached in the grandiose programme of celebrations in 1981 to mark 1,300 years of Bulgarian statehood. The driving force behind the celebrations was Zhivkov's daughter, Lyudmila, the country's cultural overlord. Heavy emphasis during the anniversary events on the fact that Bulgaria was the first Slav nation to achieve its statehood – even before Russia itself – caused some displeasure in Moscow.

The communist failure

As the examples quoted above demonstrate, Balkan communist regimes, far from 'solving' the national question, as they had proudly claimed, dealt with it even less successfully than their 'bourgeois' predecessors had done. Like them, they derived important political advantages from their manipulation of nationalism at home and in relations with other countries. But the very nationalism the communists had appropriated and had come to rely upon to help keep them in power blew up in their face in the end. In the late 1980s their own people turned on them in the name of the very same patriotism that they had been preaching. Ironically, they were found wanting not so much as communists but as the patriots they professed to be. The bill for the communists' failures in this as in other fields, however, is now being paid by their successors.

Looking back on events in the Balkans since 1945, it is no exaggeration to say that under communist rule national conflicts within the individual Balkan countries and between them have both widened and sharpened, even where – as in Yugoslavia – an attempt was made to tackle problems in a more fundamental way. One of the greatest indictments of the communist regimes in the Balkans was their failure to protect the linguistic and cultural diversity in the territories under their jurisdiction.*

The reasons for this failure have to be sought in communism's suppression of open and free debate about controversial issues and hence of free representation of interests. Without independent public criticism, the imposition from above (not always from unworthy motives) of 'official', carefully sanitized versions of past and present disputes only increased public cynicism and disbelief. This in turn encouraged, or at any rate did nothing to prevent or neutralize, the growth of prejudice and hatred, which threatened to fuel violent explosions in the future. What paved the way for those explosions, and thus also the collapse of the system itself, was communism's failure to live up to its economic promises.

---

* Yugoslavia's record was quite good here: tolerance was shown for minorities such as the Hungarians, the Albanians (from 1968 to 1988–9), and even the Gypsies; but there was a harsh response to the Croat demand for the right to separate language status.

Chapter 4

The economic black hole

When the map of Europe was redrawn after the Second World War, south-eastern Europe came to be divided into economic zones that were exactly co-terminous with its political divisions. Albania, Bulgaria, Romania and Yugoslavia had the Soviet type of command economic systems imposed on them by their new rulers. Greece and Turkey, in the Western political sphere, remained market economies, although with a strong public sector.

The pre-communist era had been by no means prosperous, let alone trouble-free, for the countries of this region. In the period between 1918 and 1941, their already serious economic disadvantages were aggravated by the fact that their numerous political troubles spilled over everywhere into the economy. As a result of conflicts between the new states that had come into being after 1918, customs barriers went up, cutting across prewar trade routes. In the 1930s the depression caused much devastation. All that the Balkans had by way of industry were some consumer-goods industries and some engineering factories in certain areas. About four-fifths of the population earned their living from agriculture. The whole region suffered from shortages of domestic capital and skilled labour.

The potential for industrialization did exist: the region had plentiful natural resources, except for energy. There were rich (though unevenly distributed) deposits of non-ferrous metals, including copper, chrome, lead and zinc in Albania, Bulgaria, Greece and Turkey – as well as in Yugoslavia, which also had plenty of bauxite. There were large oilfields in Romania, as well as some oil in Albania. There was plenty of lignite but hardly any coal or good-quality iron ore. Timber was plentiful, but the poor infrastructure and lack of capital hampered the production of other agricultural raw materials.

After 1918 all the Balkan states pursued a policy of industrialization behind high tariff barriers designed to protect domestic industry. This completed the destruction of the old Danubian economic region, the economic counterpart of the Austro-Hungarian empire. Regional customs unions were a non-starter for political reasons, mainly connected with fear of domination by the old financial centres of Vienna and Budapest. Most of the badly needed foreign capital was used for resettling refugees, stabilizing currencies, modernizing production and infrastructure, buying arms and maintaining large public-sector bureaucracies. Heavy indebtedness ended in moratoriums for Bulgaria, Greece, Romania, Turkey and Yugoslavia.

The rapid decline of agricultural prices hit these countries extremely hard. Their main trading partners imposed restrictions on agricultural imports. Closer cooperation among the countries of the area was not feasible for political reasons but also because of their lack of economic complementarity. The introduction of foreign-exchange controls meant that an ever greater proportion of trade with their main partners had to be conducted through bilateral clearing accounts.

The communist economic model

When the communists took over after the Second World War, they nationalized industry, mining, trade, banking and insurance. But the pace at which they did so varied considerably. Bulgaria and Romania were classified as former enemy countries and were subject to a degree of supervision by Allied Control Commissions – at least until the conclusion of the peace treaties in 1946–7. As part of the coalition of victorious powers, Yugoslavia and its then client-state, Albania, were free from those external restraints. In addition they were led by self-confident leaders, flushed with their revolutionary victory. So, not surprisingly, they were the first in the field, in 1946–7, with a comprehensive nationalization that took in everything down to the smallest village shop.

Over the collectivization of agriculture, too, there was a difference of pace. Again, Yugoslavia was the radical. It embarked on the project in 1949, before Bulgaria, for example, although Bulgaria was in many ways better prepared thanks to its old and well-developed cooperative tradition in agriculture and, particularly, the existence of a state marketing agency (*Hranoiznos*), founded in the pre-communist era.

This time, however, Albania did not follow suit. The two countries' economic as well as political paths had begun to diverge sharply since the

Stalin–Tito quarrel had come out into the open the year before. Albania had been intending to collectivize but was forced to wait because of the peasants' bitter resistance amid a desperate economic crisis, itself partly brought on by the break with Yugoslavia.

The politics of collectivization

It was political considerations that spurred Yugoslav leaders on to collectivize so soon, despite the fact that their economy too was in very poor shape. They felt the need to demonstrate to many of their own supporters at home that their communist orthodoxy, impugned by Soviet-bloc critics, was still intact. Unlike the other three communist-ruled Balkan states, Yugoslavia de-collectivized in 1953, after a disastrous drop in agricultural output brought on by strong passive resistance by the peasantry. But the decision to de-collectivize was preceded by a long struggle within the regime. It was necessary to overcome strong opposition from local agro-bureaucracies afraid of losing their power and jobs. Many other communists (including some in the Politburo) had been worried that 'creeping capitalism' in the countryside might lead to its restoration elsewhere. In the end, the opponents of de-collectivization lost, but not before they had exacted their revenge: the so-called 'agrarian maximum', the upper limit on private land ownership, was set very low – at 10 hectares. This decision was to handicap Yugoslav agriculture and indeed the whole economy until the country's breakup in 1991.

Even in the immediate post-1918 period, the heyday of liberal capitalism in south-eastern Europe, the state's presence was felt everywhere in the Balkan economies, though not always for the best. Corruption was endemic, particularly in Romania and Yugoslavia where inadequate, poorly paid bureaucracies, inherited from prewar Romania and Serbia, suddenly found themselves with large (and much richer) new territories to administer. Not surprisingly, financial scandals abounded. State intervention in the economy increased during the slump of the 1930s.

The economies of Bulgaria and Romania survived the Second World War in pretty good shape. In contrast, those of Yugoslavia and Albania were devastated. But all four communist-ruled Balkan countries embarked upon ambitious programmes of rapid industrialization. They were based on swift, extensive exploitation of natural resources (including the manpower 'released' from the countryside as a result of collectivization), state investment and forced savings achieved at the expense of living standards. Growth rates of communist countries soared and soon exceeded those of Greece and Turkey, which were pursuing a policy of liberalization and deregulation with financial and technical assistance from the West.

Pressure for reform

Very soon, however, the combination of poor living conditions, shortages of consumer goods and political repression led to social unrest. The central planning system itself, operating on the basis of fixed prices and state monopolies, wasted resources. By the late 1950s, the communist countries of south-eastern Europe were experiencing their first economic crisis in the shape of declining growth rates. By that time, the Soviet Union had taken the bulk of its war reparations from Bulgaria and Romania. It had also revised its pricing policy in trade with the East European countries, which had criticized it as unfair.

It was then that Bulgaria and Romania (though not Albania) embarked on their first cautious economic reforms and tried to expand their trade with the capitalist West. But neither task was easy: the former because of the limited nature of the economic reform exercise within an unreformed political environment; and the latter because, in contrast to Greece and Turkey, which had been relatively rapidly reintegrated into the world economy after the Second World War, the communist-ruled states had been absorbed into the Soviet economic sphere, at the expense of their former close trade and financial relations with the countries of Central and Western Europe.[*]

Autarky had been the main principle of Soviet-bloc policy, with only as much foreign trade – particularly with the capitalist West – as was absolutely necessary. Western Europe and the United States made their own contribution to the widening gulf between the two Europes by operating strategic trade embargoes against the East, often a convenient excuse for keeping those countries' goods out of Western markets. The Soviet Union provided its partners with energy and a wide range of raw materials in exchange for manufactured goods produced by their recently built industries. East European (including Balkan) economies were linked to the Soviet economy through bilateral trade protocols and treaties. In addition, the Council for Mutual Economic Assistance (CMEA), popularly

---

[*] In the first decade after the First World War Austria, Czechoslovakia, Germany, Italy and France had been the Balkan countries' most important export markets. But by the mid-1930s Germany had outstripped them all and become the predominant trade partner throughout the whole region, a position it retained until 1945.

known in the West as Comecon, was established in 1949. Although it originally lacked any clearly defined role, in 1962 the Soviet Union tried to develop it into a body fostering the Soviet bloc's integration through the coordination of economic and trade plans.

Even though such integration remained mostly on paper, membership of the Soviet bloc proved a serious handicap when, in the late 1950s, autarky was abandoned and Bulgaria, Romania and other East and Central European states found themselves obliged to try to expand their technological and trade cooperation with the West. For political reasons, Western embargoes imposed on trade with the Soviet Union applied to them too. The disastrous effects of their isolation within the communist-bloc ghetto were already very clear. They were seriously hampered by their limited export potential and the low quality of their industrial goods, attuned to the requirements of the 'soft' but apparently insatiable Soviet market rather than those of the extremely demanding world market. Though outside Comecon, Albania and Yugoslavia faced many of the same difficulties. All four Balkan states chose different approaches to deal with their problems. These will be examined in greater detail in the following sections, but can be summarized briefly as follows:

Bulgaria tried its luck in world (especially Middle Eastern and Mediterranean) markets, but never allowed any loosening of its extremely close Soviet connection. For a time this policy seemed to pay off but by the end of the 1980s, when the Soviet connection snapped, Bulgaria was in a critical economic condition, and an environmental ruin to boot.

The far better endowed *Romania* chose the path of economic independence, hoping to build a modern, competitive economy by relying on its good connections with both the West and the developing world. It ended up by squandering its oil assets; moreover, the regime's insistence during the 1980s on avoiding external credit at all costs while also paying off all existing debts resulted in a dramatic decline in living standards throughout Romanian society and had a disastrous effect on its infrastructure, which came to be totally neglected.

Albania was a member of Comecon from 1949 to 1962. *Yugoslavia* became an observer member in 1956. But they had other connections too. Foreign assistance on a large scale was the crucial factor for both. But it was not an unmixed blessing. Given for political reasons, that assistance – to Albania by Russia and then China, and to Yugoslavia by the West – certainly helped those countries' regimes to survive. It is no exaggeration to say that, without that tangible external backing, they would very probably have gone under. But the experiment ended badly for both countries.

In the case of Albania this was because its Stalinist leaders, though ready to change foreign partners, never even for a moment considered giving up strict centralized control. Not surprisingly, the country was in a deep crisis well before Enver Hoxha's death in 1985.

Yugoslavia came unstuck because after embarking on what were then radical reforms, it quickly went back on them. Unfortunately, extensive Western aid in the early days and even more extensive Western lending in the 1970s enabled it to live way above its means for a long time before experiencing any discomfort. By the time the pains started, it was too late – the disease had gone too far and cut too deep. In short, the cushion of Western aid, provided to shore up Yugoslavia against Soviet influence, proved to be a disservice to Yugoslavia in the longer term because it deprived it of any incentive to reform in time.

Bulgaria

Bulgaria, after managing high average annual growth rates during the early 1970s, found itself in the midst of a serious economic crisis by the end of the decade. In 1979 the so-called New Economic Mechanism was introduced – a rather timid version of the Hungarian reform programme of the same name. But the whole project, despite the great publicity given to it, remained a dead letter. At the Party Congress in 1986 there was a call for a switch from direct to indirect planning, but at the same time the party rejected the idea of market socialism. The plan's directives were eventually replaced by state orders. However, for most commodities central price setting was retained. The Congress postponed the price reform until the 1990s. This foot-dragging over economic reforms reflected strong resistance from the state and party apparat as well as enterprise managers themselves.

The regime's answer to the new troubles in the economy was an ever greater reliance on Comecon, whose share of Bulgaria's trade after 1986 exceeded 80%. The Soviet Union's share of Bulgaria's exports and imports continued at 54% throughout the 1980s. The Soviet connection had been of enormous importance from the start. Bulgaria's rapid industrialization after 1945 was carried out with Soviet technical and financial aid. Most of its machinery came from the Soviet Union, which also delivered many hundreds of plants in all sectors of industry, for instance, the Kremikovtsi and Lenin steelworks, the petrochemical complex near Burgas on the Black Sea coast and the Kozlodui nuclear power station. Over two-thirds of Bulgaria's total energy demand continued over the years to be met by the Soviet Union, with more than 90% of Bulgarian oil imports coming from there. There was a similar degree of dependence on Soviet iron ore, pig iron and cellulose. Bulgaria managed to avoid the worst consequences of the world oil price shocks in 1973–4 and 1979–80 by buying oil from the Soviet Union at prices considerably below those on the world markets. Its Soviet partner supplied generous credits during the 1970s because Bulgaria could not provide enough exports to balance the value of its energy imports from there. Like the other Balkan states, Bulgaria had in the Soviet Union a patron prepared to subsidize it for political reasons –just as the West aided Yugoslavia and made important concessions to Romania. By the same token, Albania had a succession of political patrons – first Yugoslavia, then the Soviet Union and finally China.

But Bulgaria paid a price for its dependence on the Soviet market. Most Bulgarian goods could not be sold on world markets because production was geared to lower Soviet standards, and Bulgaria had lost any incentive to try to improve its competitiveness. In 1985, shortly after Gorbachev came to power, the inefficiency of the Bulgarian economy and the low quality of Bulgarian goods were for the first time openly criticized in the Soviet media. By then, Bulgaria had amassed huge deficits in its bilateral clearing with the Soviet Union.

Desperate attempts to achieve better results in industry by hasty, ill-prepared reorganizations only aggravated the crisis. More trouble was in store. In the late 1980s acute environmental problems created by Bulgaria's forced postwar industrialization became an important subject of public debate and, as the ecological movement gathered momentum, eventually also one of the causes of the communist regime's downfall. The process started in the Danubian city of Ruse, which had become heavily polluted by chlorine gas emitted by a Romanian metallurgical plant on the other side of the river. An exhibition showing the high incidence of lung disease in Ruse over many years was mounted at the end of 1987 by an ecological group, acting with the support of the local party in Ruse but in defiance of the central authorities, which had been playing down the scale of the problem. The party admitted at first that an ecological problem existed but then took fright amid signs of mounting dissent in other spheres and broke up the group.

But agitation continued. In March 1989 some former members of the Ruse group started a movement called Ecoglasnost. Its activities combined criticism of specific unpopular projects, such as plans to divert the waters of the river Mesta and to process nuclear waste in Bulgaria, with the general argument that there could be no ecological security without a proper public discussion of, and full democratic control over, all policies affecting the environment.

Suddenly, the regime found itself under fire from an unexpected direction, being blamed, for example, for breaking its own anti-pollution regulations. In all this, there was a strong undertone of patriotic anger directed against the communists as nature despoilers. It was no accident that ecology was what finally mobilized dissent in Bulgaria. The Bulgarians, rather like the Germans, are 'green' people devoted to their beautiful countryside, the source of much fierce pride. The communists, who had so assiduously beaten the patriotic drum, were found wanting precisely as patriots.

Romania

Romania based its economic strategy under the communist regime on the hope that its natural resources (particularly oil) would allow it a fast industrial development. But the Soviet Union under Khrushchev had other ideas for Romania: it was to be Comecon's granary. Romania rejected these plans and broke away from Soviet economic control in the early 1960s in order to become an industrial power in its own right and a significant exporter to world markets. Its remarkable effort, starting in the mid-1960s, to reduce its trade dependence on the rest of Comecon, particularly the Soviet Union, met with some initial success: by the early 1970s more than 50% of its trade was with the non-communist world and about 19% of its entire trade was with the European Community. In 1976 Romania became the first Soviet-bloc country to break ranks by opening direct contacts with the European Commission in Brussels. This led in 1980 to the signing of a five-year preferential agreement with the EC. Romania's exports to West Germany, its most important trading partner in the West, exceeded imports in 1970–71, 1977 and 1980–81. Its trade with the United States and Israel also grew significantly.

For all that, the expected large boost to Romania's hard-currency earnings from sales to Western markets failed to materialize. The hope, in Romania as in many other East and Central European states, had been that success in foreign trade would serve to push growth rates sharply upwards. With that expectation Romania had accumulated a hard-currency debt of nearly $10 billion. In 1982 and 1983 it was obliged to ask its Western creditors for debt-rescheduling. Romania's export drive had failed to yield the expected results because, especially in the middle of a world recession, its products – like Bulgaria's – failed to measure up to the competitive conditions on the world market.

Romania's development strategy had proved flawed. This was partly the usual East European obsession with building costly and uneconomic steelworks and other heavy industrial plant. Thus Romania produced in the 1980s about 90% of all the capital goods it required, a policy that helped to widen the technological gap between it and the West still further. Even more important was the concentration on developing the chemical and petrochemical industries. Romania's leaders were aware that the country's oil reserves were becoming depleted, but they had hoped to compensate for this by cheap oil imports from Iran and other oil-producing Third World states, with which Romania had developed a successful trading relationship. The 1973 oil price shock destroyed the basis of this Romanian strategy. Oil prices went up but not those of oil products – at least not sufficiently to make up for the much higher crude oil prices Romania found itself obliged to pay to OPEC countries. Because of its policy of avoiding reliance on the Soviet Union for crucial products, Romania was not participating in the intra-Comecon system of preferential oil prices that the Soviet Union granted to its other partners.

The Romanian regime was well aware of its international financial vulnerability in, for example, the US Congress, where the extension of most-favoured nation (MFN) status had to be debated annually in the light of Romania's record on such issues as freedom to emigrate. But the policy-related conditions of the International Monetary Fund (IMF) were unacceptable to President Ceausescu, who instead opted in 1984 for a policy of austerity to improve the balance of payments. The Romanian government reduced its debt from $9.9 billion in 1981 to $2.5 billion in 1987 and less than $1 billion in early 1989. In April 1989, Ceausescu announced that Romania had paid off all its foreign debts, although that proved to be an empty boast.

The policy of austerity had a devastating effect on supplies to the domestic market and on Romania's production capacity. Restrictions on imports of machinery, spare parts and raw materials from the West harmed export production. The official reaction to shrinking exports was yet more restrictions on imports. Meanwhile, the workers' harsh living conditions had an adverse effect on their productivity.

In desperation, Romania was forced to turn to the Soviet Union for extra supplies of energy. But these had to be paid for in hard currency and 'hard' goods such as foodstuffs and oil-drilling equipment. Humiliatingly, in view of Romania's earlier defiance, agreements were reached with Moscow under which Romanian industry was to be modernized with the aid of Soviet capital, technology and specialists. The agreements particularly referred to Romania's ailing steel industry. The Soviet Union undertook to deliver complete plants producing oil and gas pipes to Romania. In the end, ironically, it was the spontaneous revolt by people without political leaders, hijacked by a group of disaffected communists and military leaders and joined by a few dissidents, that led to Ceausescu's overthrow and execution by firing squad in December 1989. Romania is still trying to cope with the terrible aftermath of his regime.

Albania

Albania, like Bulgaria, has been helped by foreign economic assistance provided by not one but two patrons: the Soviet Union until 1961 and then China until the break between the two regimes in 1977–8. But whereas Bulgaria was poor in resources, Albania was more like Romania in that it had been self-sufficient throughout the postwar period for most of its raw material needs. Minerals and related products accounted for three-quarters of its total exports. Albania boasted of producing 23 minerals commercially, but in reality everything except the production of chrome, copper, nickel and oil was uneconomic by market criteria if labour and other costs were properly calculated. Wages in the mines were low, and forced labour was in use until the fall of the communist regime.

Oil is Albania's oldest industry: bitumen mining had flourished even under the Romans. The modern oil industry dates back to the First World War. The Italian army, then occupying a large part of southern Albania, discovered oil deposits in several areas. Italy controlled Albania's oil industry during the interwar period and intensified production there under its occupation during the Second World War.

After the war, the industry was managed by a joint Albanian–Yugoslav concern. But because of the lack of investment and technical expertise, by 1948 output had dropped to one-fifth of what it had been six years before. After the break with Tito in 1948, the Soviet Union stepped in and provided the necessary finance and technical skills. But towards the end of the 1950s, as relations began to worsen, the Soviet Union refused to finance investment in Albania's oil industry on the grounds that it would be a waste of money, especially as the Soviet Union was beginning to prepare for the role of world exporter of oil. Moscow advised the Albanians to concentrate instead on producing vegetables, fruit and plants for industrial use within the framework of the 'international division

49

of labour' in the Soviet bloc. The country's next foreign patron, China, took a different view and supported the oil industry's expansion plans. Needless to say, the break with China in 1978 hit the industry badly.

Chrome, an essential ingredient in the production of stainless steel, made the most significant contribution to Albania's economy in the post-1945 period. In the late 1970s Albania became the world's third largest producer of chrome. Its fourteen mines, clustered along the Yugoslav border, supplied about 10% of the total world output. It was able to produce chrome (with nickel and cobalt as by-products) relatively cheaply, thanks to the ample supply of power from the hydroelectric stations begun by the Italians during the Second World War and then completed by the communist regime with Soviet assistance.

After Albania's break with the Soviet Union, China stepped in – not least because it needed an alternative source of chrome previously purchased from the Soviet Union – and financed the building of new power stations. This allowed a rapid increase in the production of chrome and copper. Nevertheless, Albania found the break painful. Between 1956 and 1960 the Soviet Union had financed 8% of all Albanian investment and a much higher proportion of industrial investment. Albania's five-year plan was geared to deliveries of machinery and equipment from the Soviet Union and Eastern Europe. Its domestic industry, agriculture and transport were based on imports from the Soviet Union. When those ceased abruptly in 1961, the lack of spare parts became an acute problem, so much so that in 1967 Albania's main engineering plants were switched to the production of spare parts.

In 1978 there came another abrupt and painful change – the break with China. This forced Albania to scrap plans for three new ferro-chrome plants designed to produce chrome for the Chinese market. Chrome exports were redirected to other markets, including those in Eastern Europe and the Soviet Union. Unfortunately for Albania, the ferro-chrome plant the Chinese had already built, at Elbasan, had 1930s technology that caused constant production problems as well as large-scale pollution. A 1990 UN report, commissioned by the Albanian government, suggested that since most of the industrial plant of this kind was completely outdated it should be closed down. The truth is that all of Albania's major industries are stuck with outdated technology that should be scrapped – it remains a symbol of the disaster inflicted on the country by the isolationist policies of the Hoxha era.

After Hoxha's death in 1985, Ramiz Alia continued his predecessor's policy of cautiously opening up contacts with a wide range of countries.

Albania increased its trade with a number of West European countries, notably West Germany. Trade with Yugoslavia, despite strained relations, continued and expanded, accounting for about 15% of Albania's total trade during the 1980s. After Yugoslavia's violent break-up in 1991, some of that trade continued – especially with Serbia and Montenegro – despite the imposition in May 1992 of UN sanctions against those two ex-Yugoslav republics for their role in the war in Bosnia. Once the war in former Yugoslavia is over, tourism could prove to be an important source of income for Albania, with its beautiful Adriatic coast and its rugged mountain scenery in the interior. But aid from the West will be needed, particularly with the development of the infrastructure.

Agriculture still employs about 60% of the labour force, the main crops being maize, sugar beet, wheat and potatoes. It was here that the regime's economic policy suffered its most spectacular defeat: the result of a combination of primitive farming methods, bad planning, inefficient management of labour and resources, and lack of investment. Throughout the 1970s Albania had to make up its grain deficit by imports. Poor distribution – lack of refrigeration facilities, transport and so on – was one of the main causes of the deeply unpopular food shortages and most of the waste. By the 1980s these difficulties had become part of a full-scale crisis that engulfed the whole economy and, ultimately, contributed to the fall of the regime.

The main factors in the economic crisis were stagnating agricultural production, failure to reach export targets, decline in the output of oil and chromite and, last but not least, population growth on a scale bound to lead to increased social tensions. Albania has an annual population growth rate of 3%, the highest in Europe. Its population doubled between 1923 and 1960 to over 1.6m and then again to 3.5m by 1980. To relieve the situation, the regime decided in March 1990 to allow private ownership of family livestock, but that led to a reduction in the output of state farms, causing a drastic cut in meat and vegetable supplies to the cities and increasing consumer discontent there.

This economic misery – made more intolerable in the eyes of many Albanians by their ability to watch Italian, Greek and Yugoslav television – was one of the sparks that ignited the revolt in 1990–91 and led to the attempted exodus to Greece, Yugoslavia and across the Adriatic to Italy and, ultimately, to the collapse of the country's communist regime.

Yugoslavia

In contrast to Romania, Yugoslavia, which was freed by the 1948 Tito–Stalin quarrel from a commercially and technologically counterproductive orientation towards the Soviet bloc, quickly developed trade links with the West and later also with the developing countries, its political partners in the non-aligned grouping. After 1945 Yugoslavia benefited from a large amount of Western (chiefly American) aid. From the point of view of Western governments, the policy of 'keeping Tito afloat' and thus denying Yugoslavia to the Soviet Union was a relatively cheap way of improving the defence of Italy and strengthening the Western Alliance's strategic position in the southern Mediterranean. The first American 'political' loan to Yugoslavia, worth $20m, was provided by the Truman administration in September 1949. By 1955, at the end of the first period of large-scale Western aid, Yugoslavia had received $600m worth of American economic assistance, of which only $55m was in the form of repayable loans. Military aid provided by the United States during the same period amounted to just under $600m. By 1960, Western aid and 'soft' credits had reached $2 billion. Later Western aid continued to be channelled mainly through international organizations, such as the IMF, the World Bank and the European Community.

Without massive Western support, Yugoslavia would have found it extremely difficult, perhaps even impossible, to maintain its independence in the early post-1948 period when it was subjected to various forms of pressure – including an economic blockade –from the Soviet Union and its allies. It was precisely Western aid that enabled the individual Yugoslav republics to pursue, within the framework of official 'Yugoslav' economic development policies, their own unstated, parallel policies. The fact that, in addition to Rijeka – Yugoslavia's largest commercial port in the northern Adriatic, which was in itself quite sufficient to carry all the country's traffic and trade – two further ports were built can be understood only in terms of these unstated but very real 'national' strategies. For example, the port of Koper – built on the small strip of the Adriatic coast just north of Rijeka that the previously land-locked Slovenia had gained after 1945 – should be seen as an expression of Slovenia's ambition to have direct access to the sea, rather than the result of an all-Yugoslav commercial calculation.

This special 'national' development strategy, more appropriate to a small sovereign state than to a republic of a federation, can be seen even more clearly in the project of a railway linking Belgrade with Bar in

Montenegro, on the southern Adriatic coast close to Albania. The project, which also included the building of a modern port at Bar, the third on the Yugoslav coast, was (quite correctly) criticized as commercially dubious, not least because of the high cost of building a railway through extremely difficult mountainous terrain. But it made sense in the context of land-locked Serbia's search, ever since the nineteenth century, for direct access to the sea. To the Serbs, what recommended the Belgrade-Bar project, discussed on and off since 1879, was that the railway avoided non-Serb (i.e., Croat or Muslim) areas and that the port was situated in Montenegro, regarded by all Serbs (and some Montenegrins) as a Serbian land. After much acrimonious debate among the republics, in which non-Serbs, predictably, objected to the Belgrade-Bar project on grounds both of cost and of commercial non-viability, the railway was eventually completed in 1976.[11]

Distinctive, 'small state' strategies have lain behind the building of most of the double capacity – steelworks and refineries as well as other factories and installations – in individual republics ever since 1945. Even in nationally homogeneous countries, there is competition for investment projects, particularly those involving public money. In multinational Yugoslavia, this competition was something quite different, bound up with the separate national agendas that continued to develop. Naturally, all this increased the cost of the Yugoslav economy, but the attraction to proponents of various 'national' projects was that not only others within Yugoslavia but the non-aligned country's rich foreign backers would help to pay for them.

Foreign backing played an important role in the preparation of Yugoslavia's economic reform in 1965. Crucial assistance came from the IMF, which provided Yugoslavia with $80m worth of special drawing rights (SDR). There was also help from the governments of Britain, Italy, France and the United States. With that reform, Yugoslavia officially embarked on the road to 'market socialism'. Imports were liberalized to provide competition for domestic enterprises. The dinar was devalued to stimulate exports. Many prices previously fixed by the state were freed. Measures to tighten credit for Yugoslav enterprises were introduced. The number of those employed in industry fell for the first time since 1952, as did industrial output. In 1966 Yugoslavia became the first communist-ruled country to allow its citizens to leave for the West. Those who left included many who had lost their jobs as a result of factory closures under the 1965 reform or who would have done so had they stayed. At the same time, the country's tourist industry was expanded. A welcome boost for the country's balance of payments was provided by hard-currency earnings from tourism and remittances sent home by the Yugoslav *Gastarbeiter* ('guest-workers').

But there was a strong political and economic backlash against the reform. The party's apparat complained of the growing power of the 'technocracy'. Behind this lay resentment of the increased independence exercised by the managers of more successful enterprises, which threatened the control of the local party bosses. Conversely, enterprises under pressure from the credit squeeze and suffering from the competition of cheaper imported goods appealed to the party for support. Growing redundancy and unemployment figures were set by the opponents of reform against the rising number of private businessmen and artisans. Student demonstrations in Belgrade in June 1968 in favour of more full-blooded socialism, under slogans such as 'Work for everyone, bread for everyone' and 'Down with the red bourgeoisie', frightened top leaders.

Tito, never a reformer himself though prepared to accept changes dictated by political necessity, sounded the retreat. Thus June 1968 marked the beginning of the end of an imaginative attempt to bring Yugoslavia over to a version of the free-market system. Competition, which so many in Yugoslavia had found uncomfortable, was soon replaced by deals among corporate interests. 'Market socialism' was replaced by 'consensus economics' (*dogovorna ekonomija*), brain-child of Edvard Kardelj, Tito's chief ideologist. It was codified in the 1974 Yugoslav federal constitution and a special self-management law in 1976.[12]

One of the consequences of the Kardelj system was the fragmentation of industry into thousands of 'self-managing' units, each with its own bureaucracy. This enabled the party to keep closer control over the 'technocrats' and the bankers in what were denounced as the 'centres of alienated power' – alienated from the party, of course. But there was a high economic price to pay; the smaller units were even more preoccupied with distributing rather than creating wealth than the previous larger ones had been.

According to some estimates, nearly two million 'self-managing' bureaucrats, two for each worker, were spawned by the Yugoslav system in the 1970s. To break up the power of the banks, which had become uncomfortably independent of the party under the reform, the banking system was reorganized into hundreds of local banks, each dominated by local political bureaucracies and serving, almost literally, as cash points for individual enterprises. Perhaps most disastrously of all, each of these banks was allowed to raise capital abroad. With plenty of petrodollars available in the aftermath of the 1973 oil crisis, and with Tito acting as Yugoslavia's credit card, the country's banks, however small and obscure, had no difficulty in raising all the capital they wanted.

In some ways, this scramble for foreign loans was inevitable, given the general shortage of capital under the Yugoslav system. Under that system, first applied in industry in the early 1950s and then extended to the entire public sector, 'self-managing' units had little or no interest in setting up subsidiaries in other parts of the country and investing in them because legally they had no direct control over those offshoots. Each of them, having been set up with the capital of the 'home' enterprise, automatically obtained the status of an autonomous 'self-managing' unit, complete with its own bureaucracy and the right to distribute income as it saw fit. The freedom to borrow abroad at what was, given Yugoslavia's inflation rate, a negative rate of interest proved irresistible. In the mid-1970s, the country went on a borrowing spree which in turn fuelled a huge investment boom. No thought was given to how those debts would be repaid. There was, at the same time, no reason for any of these Yugoslav borrowers to worry because if anything went wrong they could be sure that, in one way or another, the political bosses of their given city, district or republic would arrange their financial rescue. This situation was aptly summed up by Professor Dusan Bilandzic, one of the most acute analysts of the Yugoslav system, in his description of Yugoslavia as 'a country where profits are nationalized and losses socialized'.[13]

Here lay the roots of Yugoslavia's steadily increasing inflation. The state needed to print ever more money to support an inefficient economy, with its hordes of parasitic 'self-managing' bureaucrats, and to finance in addition a large army and a generous pensions system for Tito's wartime partisan veterans. By the end of 1980, Yugoslavia's foreign debt stood at just below $18 billion, a large enough figure to cause alarm to Western bankers and governments. These concerns were reinforced by the death in May 1980 of President Tito, who had been the guarantor of its stability for four and a half decades and its best credit card. The so-called 'Long-term Stabilization Programme', launched in July 1983 with the assistance of a large financial aid package prepared by Western governments, had no effect. Yugoslavia's economic and financial slide continued relentlessly. In 1989 its inflation reached an annual rate of 2,500%.

Hopes that Yugoslavia might at last be returning to the path of radical free-marketry first embarked upon in 1965 were raised when Ante Markovic – a former prime minister and later president of Croatia and, before that, a successful industrial manager – was appointed as Yugoslavia's federal prime minister in March 1989. In December of the same year, the Markovic government pegged the Yugoslav dinar to the Deutschmark (at a rate of 7:1) and made it freely convertible, having previously amassed more than $10 billion worth of hard-currency reserves. Inflation was halted almost immediately. Other fundamental reforms, aimed at turning Yugoslavia into a market economy and including a reform of enterprises (which effectively abolished self-management) and of the banking system (which restored the independence of the banks from local interests) were also launched.

But it became evident in 1990 that there was no political consensus among the republics for the Markovic programme, which remained stalled as a result of strong opposition from various quarters. Croatia and Slovenia broadly supported the prime minister's policies, but they feared that a strengthening of the federal centre, agreed to on economic grounds, could subsequently, under a different prime minister, be used to regain central political control as well. Much the strongest opposition came from Serbia, Yugoslavia's largest but also economically most troubled republic. Serbia objected to Markovic's import liberalization policy and his drastic squeeze on credit to loss-making enterprises, seeing both – quite correctly – as a threat to its bankrupt industries.

Even before the outbreak of war in Slovenia and Croatia in the summer of 1991, there had emerged an important new element in the situation – a certain 'Yugoweariness' in the West, which manifested itself in a reluctance to undertake unconditional financial rescues of Yugoslavia. Some of the old readiness to help a country in which so much Western effort had been invested over the years did survive, but nothing was unconditional any longer. Help had to be justified in each individual instance as against other claims on Western resources. This reflected, more clearly than anything else, Yugoslavia's – but also the whole area's – loss of strategic importance in the post-Cold War era. For all four Balkan countries it was an ominous development.

A Balkan ghetto?

Politically motivated aid in a variety of forms had sustained all the four Balkan countries considered here throughout the post-1945 period. That aid had helped make up for the serious deficiencies of communist economic policies. It had helped the local regimes to get away without any serious reforms and thus to stay more securely in power and, ultimately, postpone the day of reckoning. With the collapse of the post-1945 political order in the region, that day has now arrived. Tragically, at the very time when really fundamental change is at long last possible (unlike previous bouts of tinkering with the old communist system), and when these countries desperately need foreign investment and technical aid to help them with the transition from the state-dominated economic system to the one where the free market plays the dominant role, international interest in them has waned.

This is, of course, in the first place due to the war in former Yugoslavia, which has severely disrupted the economies of the whole region and made the Balkans something of a no-go area for world business. It is true that, once the fighting in Bosnia is over and provided a reasonably durable political settlement emerges, there will be some outside business interest in participating in the reconstruction of war-torn Bosnia and Croatia and in the rebuilding of the whole region's badly neglected infrastructure. But there will be intense competition for Western goodwill over matters such as debt repayment and trade concessions from states regarded as 'better bets' to succeed: the Baltic republics, the Czech Republic, Hungary, Poland and, not least, from eastern Germany. It is into those countries' economies that the bulk of Western capital investment will probably continue to flow, rather than into the more questionable Balkan region. The relatively bleak economic outlook will make the political reshaping of the Balkans far more complicated and dangerous. It is a vicious circle, for it will be the area's success in carrying out its own political restructuring reasonably peacefully and achieving a degree of political stability fairly quickly that will determine its chances of attracting foreign investment. And the omens are not good in either the political or the economic field, for the two are inextricably linked.

All four Balkan states started by sharing the main political, economic and social problems involved in the transition from communism to postcommunism. But there was one crucial difference between Yugoslavia on the one side and Albania, Bulgaria and Romania on the other. In Yugoslavia, it was not only the communist political and economic system that was being dismantled but also the multinational state itself.

Both Bulgaria and Romania are having to cope with the difficult task of making a go of their economies while at the same time trying to satisfy their respective Hungarian and Turkish minorities' demands for human rights and political representation and not allowing the extreme Bulgarian and Romanian nationalists to exploit any backlash among the majority population against such concessions. This will be hard enough, particularly given the serious economic situation in both countries, but in the foreseeable future both Bulgaria and Romania will almost certainly remain sovereign states within their present borders.

Albania's transition to democracy is made more difficult by its extreme poverty – one of the legacies of an ultra-isolationist brand of communism – and by its lack of a democratic tradition. Although there has been progress in the economic field, many problems remain. Albania's reformers face opposition from extreme nationalists over the granting of human and political rights to the country's Greek minority, which was subjected for decades to considerable cultural repression by the communist regime. The reformers' position is not made any easier by Greece's attempt to bully post-communist Albania over its admittedly less-than-perfect human rights record for its own foreign policy purposes and to make political capital at home by appearing to champion fellow-Greeks abroad. Albania's vulnerability over this issue will play a role in its choice of foreign policy partners.

Nevertheless, despite all these problems, no one is actively challenging the existence of Albania as a state, nor is the existence of Bulgaria or Romania being called into question. Unlike them, Yugoslavia not only experienced the collapse of its political and economic system but actually collapsed as a state. Its violent disintegration in 1991 has affected everyone in the area. It is no exaggeration to say that the future shape of the Balkans largely depends on how the successor states of former Yugoslavia ultimately arrange themselves – both with one another and with outside partners. The next chapter analyses the deeper reasons for the political crisis and the military conflict that led to Yugoslavia's break-up and speculates on the final outcome.

Chapter 5

Yugoslavia's road to war

There were many reasons why Yugoslavia broke up in 1991–2, but the principal one was that its bigger nations and key interest groups (notably the Yugoslav People's Army, or JNA) had come to reject it – at least in the form it then was – as not measuring up to their very different and often mutually exclusive needs and aspirations.

There had of course always been dissatisfaction in, and with, Yugoslavia. But for a long time such dissatisfaction was of no political significance. A strong glue held Yugoslavia in one piece for three and a half decades after the Second World War. It had several ingredients. One was Tito, a charismatic leader at the head of a Communist Party and an army personally loyal to him as the man who had brought them to power. That was particularly true of the Yugoslav army. Another factor of cohesion was the fear, shared by the majority of the population, communists and non-communists alike, of Yugoslavia falling under Soviet domination. Yet another cohesive element was the country's steadily rising prosperity which, during the last two decades of Tito's rule, created a mood of optimism and hope. Last but by no means least, there was the 'external factor'. Whatever Yugoslavia's own citizens thought of their state – whether or not they liked it or wanted it – the outside world did. In the eyes of the West, an independent Yugoslavia keeping Russia at arm's length was an asset during the Cold War. To keep it afloat – and thus out of Moscow's sphere – the West was prepared to reach into its pocket. For its part, Moscow too saw its own interests best served by an independent but still communist Yugoslavia. It trusted Tito to keep it that way.

But, just when the world had convinced itself that under Tito's leadership Yugoslavia had become a permanent fixture on the international scene, the glue holding the federation together began to dissolve. Tito

Map 4 Yugoslavia 1945–91

© Vladimir P. Kušić 1991

AUSTRIA

HUNGARY

ROMANIA

BULGARIA

GREECE

ALBANIA

ITALY

SLOVENIA

Ljubljana

Koper

Rijeka

Zagreb

CROATIA

Knin

VOJVODINA

Novi Sad

Belgrade

SERBIA

BOSNIA & HERCEGOVINA

Sarajevo

Vrbas

Drina

SANDZAK

MONTE NEGRO

Titograd

Bar

KOSOVO

Priština

Skopje

MACEDONIA

ADRIATIC SEA

miles

km

20 40 60 80 100 200

50 100

Republican boundary

Provincial boundary

died in May 1980, a few weeks before his 88th birthday. Not long after that, Yugoslavia got into serious financial difficulties as its international creditors began to call in the debts it had amassed under Tito, particularly in the last decade of his rule. By the second half of the 1980s, the Cold War was ending and with it also Yugoslavia's key strategic role in the East–West confrontation that had to be propped up whatever the cost. Internally, the end of the Cold War finally removed the sense of external danger that had been an important factor of cohesion ever since 1948. Another, the Communist Party of Yugoslavia, already divided organizationally into six republican and two provincial parties (Kosovo and Vojvodina), and also split along ideological lines into reformist and 'dogmatic' wings, broke up at an abortive Congress in Belgrade in January 1990.

What all this meant was that, for the first time in its history, Yugoslavia's future was for its citizens alone to decide, without any external interference or assistance. But they disagreed profoundly about what should happen next. Ironically, the one thing all of Yugoslavia's nations shared was their firm conviction that each and every one of them had had a particularly raw deal in Yugoslavia.

The Serbs

The most vocal complainants, particularly since the mid-1960s, had been the Serbs, Yugoslavia's largest nation (comprising 36% of the total population, according to the 1981 census,[14] but only 35% according to the provisional results of the March 1991 one). The Serb case against Tito's federal Yugoslavia was most clearly set out in a draft Memorandum prepared in 1985–6 by a working group of the Serbian Academy of Sciences in Belgrade. This document put forward three main objections to Titoist Yugoslavia from the Serbian point of view:

(1) The federal government's alleged discriminatory policy against Serbia in the economic field, and the predominance in economic decision-making ever since 1945 of Croatia and Slovenia, the two western republics.

(2) The division of the Serbian republic of the Yugoslav federation into three parts under Tito's 1974 Constitution: Serbia proper and the autonomous provinces of Vojvodina and Kosovo. These two provinces were allowed direct participation in decision-making at the federal level, bypassing Serbia, which made them *de facto* republics.

(3) The allegedly anti-Serb policy pursued in Kosovo by Albanian 'separatists' and 'irredentists' (with support from non-Serb republics), which the authors blamed for the steady exodus of Serbs.

The Memorandum also alleged that the Serbs in Croatia were being discriminated against and subjected to a form of *de facto* assimilation. The Memorandum's authors saw as the guiding principle behind all these policies the slogan 'strong Yugoslavia, weak Serbia' and called for its reversal, especially the abolition of the 1974 Constitution as the embodiment of that principle. The document's main conclusion was that under Tito (who was part Croat and part Slovene) and his Slovene second-in-command, Edvard Kardelj, the Serbs had been treated unfairly in Yugoslavia.[15]

Behind this Serbian backlash against Tito's Yugoslavia lay an almost palpable nostalgia for the first, royalist, Yugoslavia. This was echoed in numerous articles and books that followed the Memorandum's publication. The general Serbian view that emerged then was that, despite the pre-1941 kingdom's many imperfections (not least of which was the fact that it was not called Serbia), it was nevertheless a state the Serbs could identify with and call their own, both because all the Serbs were within its borders and because they were playing the role of the leading nation.

The Serbian Academy's Memorandum is now regarded as a seminal document and the modern equivalent of the famous *Nacertanije*, the national programme for a 'Greater Serbia' prepared in 1844 by Ilija Garasanin, Serbia's Minister of the Interior. According to Garasanin, that state was to be the successor to the short-lived fourteenth-century Serbian state of King Stefan Dusan, and would take in all Serbs. But Garasanin did not mean only the Serbs (and the Montenegrins, who were Orthodox like the Serbs and traditionally regarded by the Serbs as part of the Serbian nation), but also the Croats, the Bosnian Muslims and the Macedonians.

If the Memorandum provided a theoretical basis for Serbian reassertion in Yugoslavia in the post-Tito period, action was provided by Slobodan Milosevic, who was appointed Serbia's party leader in 1986, the year of the Memorandum's publication. Milosevic's background was that of a communist apparatchik who surprised everyone by turning himself into a brilliant populist politician with an ear for the frustrations of the Serbs and the knack of exploiting them politically. He found the starting-point for his campaign of Serbian reassertion among the Serb minority in Kosovo. In 1389 the Serbs in Kosovo Polje had suffered a heavy defeat at the hands of the Turks that eventually led to their loss of independence and subjection to Ottoman rule for the next five centuries.

Recovery of Kosovo became the Serbs' constant hope and aim. By 1912, however, when Serbia did regain Kosovo from the Turks, the bulk of the Serbs there had left, whereas the number of Albanians had increased.

Principally because of the Albanians' high birth-rate, this demographic trend had accelerated. The 1961 census, for example, listed 646,605 Albanians living in Kosovo (67.2% of the total population). By the time of the 1981 census – the last complete one – their number had increased to 1,226,736 (77.4% of the total). According to the provisional estimates in March 1991 (Kosovo Albanians boycotted the census), their number had gone up to 2 million in the province and 2.4 million in the whole of Yugoslavia. Meanwhile, the number of Serbs in Kosovo had fallen from 227,016 in 1961 (18.4% of the province's total population) to 209,498 in 1981 (13.2% of the total). By 1991 the Serb proportion of Kosovo's population had dropped to well below 10%, while the Albanian one had leapt to more than 90%.

A second factor was steady Serbian emigration from the province. The Serbs blamed this on local Albanian 'terror', which – they claimed – was aimed at driving out all the Serbs and creating an 'ethnically pure' Kosovo. The Albanian response was that Kosovo's Serbs were actually glad to be able to get out of the province, the Yugoslav federation's poorest region, with a high unemployment rate and bleak economic prospects. This view was supported by impartial observers.[16]

Milosevic encouraged the mass media in Serbia – particularly Belgrade Television – to step up the dissemination of allegations about the Albanian 'terror' with the aim of radicalizing Serb opinion and building a new and aggressive populist movement. He paid a dramatic visit to the province in the spring of 1987 and met the local Serbs, who complained to him that the ethnic Albanians had maltreated them and that the local (mostly ethnic Albanian) police had failed to give them proper protection. Milosevic promised the Kosovo Serbs that 'nobody would ever beat them again'. In the autumn of 1987 he used their alleged plight to attack the previous leadership in Serbia (including his own mentor, Ivan Stambolic), for having been 'too weak' on Kosovo, and to carry out a thorough purge in the Serbian Communist Party and thus consolidate his own power.

In response to Milosevic's demands for more 'law and order' in Kosovo, a federal police unit composed of detachments from several Yugoslav republics was dispatched there in October 1987. Throughout the summer of 1988 Milosevic's supporters, 'bussed' from Kosovo and other parts of Serbia, staged a series of huge rallies in various parts of the republic. In October 1988, after one such rally in Novi Sad, the capital of the Vojvodina province, a pro-Milosevic group was installed in power there. After several similar rallies in Montenegro's capital, Titograd (now once again Podgorica, its name before 1945), a pro-Milosevic group came to power there, too, in January 1989.

In Kosovo, meanwhile, unrest continued among the Albanian majority over the increasing police repression. A general strike in February 1989 was followed by a hunger strike by miners in the Trepca lead and zinc mining complex in protest against the impending constitutional changes, which would deprive the province of its autonomy and effectively reintegrate it fully into Serbia. On 23 March 1989 Kosovo's assembly gave its reluctant assent to the constitutional changes demanded by Belgrade; Vojvodina (fully under the control of pro-Milosevic forces) had already done so. On 28 March Serbia's assembly adopted the constitutional amendments, giving the Serbian authorities in Belgrade direct control over Kosovo's police, courts and territorial defence – with an extra amendment thrown in enabling the Serbian assembly to take decisions affecting Kosovo without first consulting that province's own assembly. In September 1991 Kosovo's Albanian leaders, including many members of the by then forcibly dissolved Kosovo provincial assembly, met secretly and declared Kosovo an independent republic. But Belgrade responded with increased repression and split Kosovo into two administrative units, called Kosovo and Metohija.

These events raised Milosevic's popularity to unprecedented heights with the Serbs – not just among those in Serbia proper and the provinces of Kosovo and Vojvodina but also among the *Precani* Serbs in Bosnia and Croatia. Milosevic's success in presenting himself as the champion of all Serbs throughout Yugoslavia was an important factor in his electoral victory at Serbia's first multi-party election in December 1990. He was re-elected President of Serbia with a large majority of votes. Under him, the Socialist Party of Serbia (the renamed Communist Party) also won, relying on its tight control of the media, some ballot-rigging and, last but not least, the fact that ethnic Albanians in Kosovo boycotted the election *en masse*, giving Milosevic a number of extra, totally uncontested, seats in the Serbian assembly in Belgrade.

Among non-Serbs – notably the Slovenes and the Croats – the ever more violent Milosevic-led campaign of Serbian assertion caused widespread alarm. With Milosevic seemingly hell-bent on restoring the Serbs' old hegemony in Yugoslavia, through the use of force if necessary, the question facing non-Serbs was whether they could afford to stay under the same Yugoslav roof with the Serbs.

The Slovenes

This cooling-off towards Yugoslavia was particularly striking among the Slovenes, for so long fervent supporters of the federation. Slovene doubts, which had started in the 1960s, turned into total disenchantment by the late 1980s. Various factors, some of them going back a long time, played a role in this volte-face.

One of the earliest reasons for Slovene misgivings was the revival in the early 1960s of the idea of 'integral Yugoslavism' (*jugoslovenstvo*). This was inspired by the new Yugoslav Communist Party programme adopted at the Party Congress in 1958, which envisaged an eventual merging of separate national cultures into a single Yugoslav culture within the context of a Yugoslav patriotism that would transcend individual national loyalties.

This campaign was taken seriously because it was led by people like Dobrica Cosic, a Serbian writer then close to Aleksandar Rankovic, the hardline head of the Yugoslav secret police and former party cadre secretary. Rankovic, who was himself a Serb, was thought at that time likely to succeed Tito. To the Slovenes and Yugoslavia's other non-Serbs, this concept of *jugoslovenstvo* looked suspiciously like a new version of King Alexander's attempt after 1929 to create a hybrid 'Yugoslav nation' – which in reality turned out to be Serbianization under another name.

As a small nation owing its survival principally to the fact that it had managed to keep its culture, notably its national language and literature, Slovenia was not having any of that. With the tacit support of the Slovene Party's Central Committee, the concept of 'Yugoslavism' was attacked in *Borba*, the chief party newspaper, by Dusan Pirjevec, a well-known Slovene Party intellectual. Cosic replied, and a long and bitter polemic followed. It ended in a draw because both Cosic and Pirjevec had their highly-placed backers in the party. But the purpose had been achieved. Slovenia had made its point.

A re-run of this controversy, which clearly demonstrated the Slovenes' sensitivity over their national culture, took place in the early 1980s. It was over plans for an all-Yugoslav 'core' educational curriculum in all secondary schools for subjects such as history and literature. Thanks largely to strong Slovene opposition, the project – like the earlier *jugoslovenstvo* issue – was dropped amid strong polemics between Serbian and Slovene intellectuals.

Slovenia had other important grievances, most of them a mixture of political and economic considerations. One of the biggest was the

Serbian occupation and re-annexation of Kosovo. This was deeply disapproved of on political grounds but even more irritating was the fact that the huge financial burdens of the operation were borne by the whole of Yugoslavia (including Slovenia) even though only Serbia decided policy towards Kosovo. With only 8% of the total population of Yugoslavia, Slovenia in the 1980s accounted for a third of Yugoslavia's gross national product as well as a quarter of its total exports. It demanded – but failed to obtain – a reduction in the large (and constantly rising) federal budget, in which the biggest items were expenditure on Yugoslavia's large federal army and civil service. Then there was the growing, politically motivated Serbian anti-reform obstruction on the economic front from the mid-1980s onwards, including trade boycotts against Slovenia and special tariffs on Slovene goods to punish the republic for allowing its media to publish critical items on Kosovo – including those contributed by Albanians from Kosovo. To crown it all, there was the monetary 'coup' in December 1990, in which the Serbian government 'helped itself' via the National Bank of Serbia to $1.7 billion worth of money from the Yugoslav National Bank – the bulk of the fresh money supply earmarked for the whole of Yugoslavia for 1991.

The Slovenes' greatest concern, however, was the looming threat of the imposition of a new, strongly Serbian-flavoured centralist regime in Belgrade presided over by Milosevic. Many Slovenes – including a good many communists – feared that, under such a dispensation, not only would Slovenia's autonomy be curtailed but further democratization would also be blocked. For in Slovenia in the 1970s and early 1980s, democratic initiatives aimed at achieving greater Slovene autonomy in Yugoslavia had been matched by 'non-national' initiatives arising from concerns with the environment, anti-militarism, sexual freedom, and other 'civil society' issues. Alarm-bells started ringing in Slovenia in June 1988 when the army staged a trial in Ljubljana against a group including Janez Jansa, a writer on the liberal weekly *Mladina*, on the trumped-up charges of divulging military secrets. *Mladina* had angered the Yugoslav army leadership by exposing the corruption of leading generals, including that of Admiral Branko Mamula, the defence minister, and by attacking Yugoslavia's large arms sales to oppressive regimes such as that of Colonel Mengistu in Ethiopia.

What was new about those Slovene grievances, some of which went back a long time, was Slovenia' feeling not only that it would like to cut loose from Yugoslavia but that it could now actually afford to do so. It no longer saw the old Yugoslav haven as indispensable for national survival. For many years Slovenia had enjoyed excellent bilateral relations with its two prosperous and peaceful neighbours, Austria and Italy. Since 1978 there had also been varied and successful multilateral cooperation within the framework of the *Alpe-Jadran* (Alpen-Adria) regional grouping, an originally Italian idea for a 'working community' that included, in addition to Croatia and Slovenia, four northern regions of Italy, five Austrian *Länder*, Bavaria and the three western regions of Hungary.

Slovenia's exit from Yugoslavia was accomplished in several stages. On 2 July 1990 its National Assembly, following the example of the Baltic republics in the Soviet Union, adopted a declaration on sovereignty which stipulated that Yugoslavia's federal constitution would henceforth apply to Slovenia only if it did not conflict with Slovene laws. It was also announced that Slovenia would develop its own foreign and defence policies. In September the Slovene government brought the republic's territorial defence force under its own peacetime control. At a referendum on 23 December 1990 an overwhelming majority voted to empower the government to proclaim an 'independent and sovereign' Slovenia, failing the successful conclusion within a six-month period of an agreement among all the six Yugoslav republics for the restructuring of the federation.

The culmination of the process was Slovenia's declaration of independence on 25 June 1991. The declaration[17] noted that 'under the hitherto effective constitutional order, the Republic of Slovenia had the status of a sovereign state which exercised part of its sovereign rights in the Socialist Federal Republic of Yugoslavia' but went on to note that, since the SFRY no longer functioned as a 'legally-regulated state', Slovenia was now an independent state; the SFRY constitution was no longer in force in Slovenia; and Slovenia had taken over all the rights and obligations which under the former Slovene and SFRY Constitutions had been transferred to the agencies of the SFRY.

Slovenia's bid for independence was not unopposed. The Yugoslav People's Army intervened, but unsuccessfully. Within a matter of days and at the cost of only a handful of casualties and relatively little material damage, Slovenia managed to beat the army back. It was helped by the quality of its leadership, its national and political homogeneity and, perhaps most importantly, its geographical position in the far northwestern corner of Yugoslavia next to Austria and Italy. It was also helped by the JNA's all-too-evident underestimation of the Slovenes' determination and ability to fight back.

The Croats

For the Croats, too, Yugoslavia had at one time seemed a welcome prospect. In the nineteenth century and the early years of the twentieth, Croat intellectuals and churchmen were the most enthusiastic advocates of the idea of a union of all Southern Slavs. At the end of the First World War, grave danger to their national territory loomed from the south. Italy had been promised, under the 1915 Treaty of London, most of Croatia's northern Adriatic coast (including the offshore islands) as an inducement to join the war on the Entente's side. At the end of 1918, in the wake of Austria-Hungary's collapse, Italy was thus busy occupying the territories promised to it. For the Croats, union in a new Southern Slav state with Serbia, a member of the victorious Entente coalition, seemed the best protection against these Italian claims.

But post-1918 Yugoslavia proved a bitter disappointment to the Croats. This was partly because the government in Belgrade had failed to stop Italy from acquiring much of the territory promised under the Treaty of London. A deeper reason was that in Yugoslavia Croatia lost the autonomous status it had enjoyed up to 1918 as one of the 'historic' nations of the Habsburg empire. Rather late in the day, in August 1939, on the eve of the outbreak of war, prospects for Serb–Croat accommodation seemed to improve. Croatia became a separate unit called *Banovina Hrvatska* – though with less autonomy than it had had in Austria-Hungary before 1918. That arrangement was supported by Croatia's Serbs, who had grown to mistrust their fellow-Serbs running the government in Belgrade and had come to feel that their interests would be better protected by the authorities in Zagreb, the Croatian capital.

However, the new autonomous Croat unit within Yugoslavia was rejected by most of the political parties in Serbia and the bulk of the Serbian intelligentsia. This rejection echoed the vehement opposition of the Serbian Orthodox church in 1937 to the proposed concordat with the Vatican, which would have given the Roman Catholic church equality of status with the Serbian Orthodox church. The public demonstrations led by the Serbian Orthodox Patriarch had forced the government to give up the idea.

The lack of full recognition of traditional Croat identity and national autonomy in the unitary Yugoslav state aggravated the Croats' sense of insecurity with regard to the Serbs. The Croats felt directly threatened by the possibility of Serbianization (disguised as campaigns for 'Yugoslavism'). Ironically, the very fact that the Croats and the Serbs were linguistically close only increased the Croats' sense of insecurity – with reason, for linguistic closeness generally facilitates assimilation.

There was a basis for the Croats' fear of assimilation. The founder of modern Serb national ideology, the nineteenth-century linguistic reformer Vuk Stefanovic Karadzic, defined as Serbs all those who spoke the central-south Slavic dialect (*stokavian*) – among them the vast majority of Croats and Bosnian Muslims. Vuk's ideas, which before 1918 had also been accepted by many prominent pro-Yugoslav Croat linguists, served as one of the bases of the political concept adopted after 1918 of a single 'Yugoslav' nation made up of three 'tribes': the Croats, the Serbs and the Slovenes – at that time the Macedonians and the Bosnian Muslims were not recognized as separate nations. After 1918 an ever-increasing number of Croats came to see Vuk's 'unitarist' ideology as a back door to the 'Serbianization' of the country's non-Serb Slavs.

Despite the Croats' substantial participation in the ranks of Tito's victorious anti-Axis guerrilla forces, the Croats felt ill at ease in his post-1945 Yugoslav federation. One explanation for this was the dominant position of Croatian Serbs, which was out of proportion to their numbers within Croatia. Many of them had joined the Tito forces to escape extermination under Ante Pavelic's wartime quisling state but the Serbs' over-representation in the communist republic's *nomenklatura* continued long after the war. Though constituting only 11.6% of Croatia's population, the Serbs made up 19.4% of all party members in 1987. The imbalance was even higher in the permanent party apparat, the police, the Yugoslav army and the senior ranks of state administration. This state of affairs suited Tito: the ultra-loyal and strongly communist Croatian Serbs helped keep the Croats under control. Moreover, by apparently favouring Croatian Serbs he was trying to appease those in Serbia, most of whom had supported the royalist guerrilla leader Draza Mihailovic during the Second World War (see Chapter 2) and could not forgive Tito for bringing him to trial and execution.

All manifestations of Croat national feeling were viewed with great suspicion by Croatia's Serbs and were too readily branded as 'separatism', 'nationalist extremism' and a threat to the official doctrine of 'brotherhood and unity' among all of Yugoslavia's nations. That happened in 1967 with the so-called 'Language Declaration', signed on behalf of 18 Croat cultural institutions by 140 prominent scholars, writers and other intellectuals. The Declaration demanded the return to the position during the wartime partisan struggle and immediately after 1945 when full constitutional recognition was given (even on Yugoslav banknotes) to four languages – Croatian, Macedonian, Serbian and Slovene. The Declaration called for all the federal laws to be published in these four languages (at that time, only three were recognized officially: Macedonian, Serbo-Croat and Slovene). It also demanded the use of standard Croatian in schools and in the mass media throughout the republic, instead of Serbo-Croatian, which was rejected by most Croats as a political language and a manifestation of official Yugoslav 'unitarism'.

The Declaration caused a bitter public row and many of its signatories were expelled from the party. In a bizarre sequel to this political-linguistic controversy, an orthographic handbook produced in 1971 by leading Croatian grammarians for use in schools and offices was branded as dangerously 'chauvinist' and 'separatist' by the authorities the following year. They ordered the entire printing of 40,000 copies to be burnt – as if it were an urban guerrilla handbook rather than an orthography text.

This happened at the height of the purge in 1971–2 when President Tito, acting partly in response to demands by senior Croatian Serbs, crushed the 'Croatian Spring', a political and national revival that had begun after the sacking of Aleksandar Rankovic and other senior secret police officials in 1966. The purge was part of a larger all-Yugoslav crackdown on 'liberals' and 'technocrats', but was much harsher in Croatia than anywhere else in Yugoslavia. It had a stultifying effect on national political and cultural life in Croatia – just as the suppression of the 1968 'Prague Spring' had done in Czechoslovakia. This prolonged, systematic repression, which earned Croatia the title of a 'silent republic', had a number of negative long-term effects.

One of the most harmful was the deepening of mistrust between the majority Croat population and the republic's Serb minority, which destroyed the possibility of reviving their pre-1941 anti-Belgrade alliance. Perhaps inevitably, the Croats' instinctive response to Tito's purge, which they saw as a full-scale attack on their basic national identity, was to concentrate on defending those things which seemed to be in particular danger, such as the national coat of arms and flag, and the Croat language and culture. Unfortunately, there was nothing there for Croatia's Serbs to identify with. They felt left out and – with memories of Pavelic's extremist brand of Croatian nationalism still fresh in their minds – apprehensive about the future.

This growing Serb–Croat rift, set against the background of increasing Croat rejection of Yugoslavia, was one of the main reasons why there was no joint Croat–Serb struggle for democracy and civil rights in Yugoslavia. While more and more Croats were coming to reject Yugoslavia, most Serbs (including supporters of democratic change) were still taking Yugoslavia's continued existence for granted. Among the Croats, the increasing emphasis on the purely 'national' aspects of the struggle against the regime led to less emphasis being placed on the aims of democracy, pluralism and civil rights. (This was in contrast to the situation, for example, in the nationally homogeneous Slovenia, where the fight for national autonomy went hand-in-hand with that for democracy.)

The Croats' powerful, long-suppressed national frustrations found delayed expression in the first multi-party election in April/May 1990. It resulted in an overwhelming victory for the right-of-centre Croatian Democratic Union (*Hrvatska Demokratska Zajednica* or HDZ), which presented itself to the electorate as 'the most Croat of all political parties'. Nevertheless, its leader, Dr Franjo Tudjman, a historian and a former Tito general and, more recently, a dissident who had been imprisoned for his views, pursued a cautious course towards Yugoslavia.

On 4 October 1990 Croatia proposed, jointly with Slovenia, a 'confederal' model for Yugoslavia as a loose grouping of states modelled on the European Community, with a single market and common foreign policy and common armed forces – although the republics would also have their own forces. The proposal was summarily rejected by Serbia. On 19 May 1991 Croatia held a referendum at which voters were asked two questions. The first was whether a sovereign and independent Croatia, guaranteeing cultural autonomy and all the civic rights to the Serbs and other nationalities living in Croatia, could – together with the other republics – join a confederation of sovereign states. The vote in favour was 93%. The other proposition – that Croatia should remain a federal republic of Yugoslavia – was rejected by 92% of voters. On 25 June 1991 Croatia proclaimed itself a sovereign state preparatory to declaring independence if agreement over a loose confederation was not reached.

Since the advent of Milosevic, with the spectre of revived Serbian hegemonism allied to a version of populist communism stalking the land, the Croats' rejection of Yugoslavia had become total. But it was tempered by the realization that new and serious problems were being caused by the Croatian Serbs' vehement rejection of a more independent status for Croatia within a Yugoslav confederation, let alone full independence. Many Croat Serbs, particularly those of the older generation that remembered the Second World War, said that they feared persecution in a Croatia no longer supervised from Belgrade – a fear which the triumphalist Tudjman government did little or nothing to dispel. But there was also the Croatian Serbs' not unjustified fear that, under the new, non-communist Croat government, those who belonged to the old *nomen-*

klatura would lose jobs, privileges, subsidies and other benefits they had received from the communist regime – not least in the wake of the 1971–2 mass sackings of 'disloyal' Croats who in many cases had been replaced by 'loyal' Serbs.

Croatian Serbs began to show their opposition to any change in the status quo in Croatia even before the multi-party elections in spring 1990. Mass rallies attended by Serbs from all over Yugoslavia were held in the Knin region of southern Croatia close to the Adriatic coast against the (still communist) Croat local authorities in June 1989, to coincide with continuing pro-Milosevic rallies held in Serbia. Secret arming of local Serbs began at the same time. In August 1990, following the HDZ's election victory in Croatia in May, an armed rebellion began against the new authorities. Having conducted their own referendum on the question of autonomy, the Serbs of 11 predominantly Serb districts proclaimed themselves an autonomous region called *Krajina* (from the name *Vojna Krajina* – Military Frontier – given by the Habsburgs to army-run districts along the borders of the Ottoman empire, which had included some of this region). The well-armed and coordinated Knin irregulars repeatedly cut rail and road links between Zagreb and the Adriatic coast. Another Serb armed uprising began in Slavonia in eastern Croatia in February 1991. Supported openly by the Milosevic regime in Belgrade (and more discreetly by senior Yugoslav army commanders in Croatia), the Krajina Serbs proclaimed themselves on 1 April 1991 a part of Serbia, a step which Serbia's assembly in Belgrade took note of but did not formally acknowledge.

The Croatian authorities tried to act to quell this rebellion but each time Croatian police were sent in, the Yugoslav federal army moved in as well, claiming it was 'stopping' ethnic clashes. There was an important factor in play here: although the Yugoslav army was a conscript army drawn from all the nations and national minorities of Yugoslavia, an estimated 70% of its officers were Serbs. By that time, too, many Croat, Slovene and other non-Serb conscripts had either left the army or been sent to Serbia and Montenegro.

Unlike Slovenia, which had managed to retain about 40% of its territorial army weapons, Croatia had been stripped of all such weaponry and equipment at the time of the political changeover in May 1990. They had been quietly impounded by the Yugoslav army with the aid of the Serbs in the republic's *nomenklatura* – as were most of the arms of the Croat police reserve. In the wake of the Serb rebellion in August 1990, Croatia hastily trained, in addition to extra police, some 20,000 gendarmes (*specijalci*), arming them with light weapons, including about 10,000 AK-47 automatic rifles and ammunition, bought abroad (mostly from the discarded stocks of the disbanded Communist Party militia, the 'Factory Guard', in Hungary).

Why did the Tudjman administration, despite the overwhelmingly pro-independence mood in Croatia, hesitate so long over declaring independence from Yugoslavia, pressing instead for a confederal option? The reason was Croatia's vulnerability to the combined Serb–army pressure. (In Slovenia, by contrast, with its 90.5% ethnic Slovene population, there was no sizeable hostile 'Fifth Column' to oppose and sabotage independence, and, just as important, no common border with Serbia.) That caution, arising out of an acute sense of vulnerability, explains why the Croats, having declared their independence on 25 June, did not try to take over the control posts on Croatia's only international border – that with Hungary. Just such an action by the Slovenes on their borders with Austria and Italy was used by the Yugoslav army as a pretext to intervene. Clearly the Croats calculated that by avoiding this kind of provocation they could stave off the army's retaliation for their declaration of independence. But in the end, President Tudjman's circumspection did not prevent Croatia from becoming involved in a war with a far stronger enemy.

The 'dirty war' in Croatia, which had started in the summer of 1990, developed into a full-scale war in August 1991. It took the form of a number of concerted attacks by Serb irregulars, trained, armed and increasingly openly supported by the Yugoslav army. By the time fighting had stopped in January 1992, about a third of Croatia was under Serbian control. According to the most authoritative study so far of the war in Croatia,[18] the war had caused 18,000 confirmed Croat casualties by the end of 1991 (of whom 1,448 were soldiers killed in action and over 10,000 wounded) and some 14,000 missing, many of whom are reckoned to be dead. According to the United Nations High Commissioner for Refugees, the number of registered displaced persons and refugees in Croatia in October 1991 totalled 379,908, although with up to 10% more unregistered, the total came to around 418,000.[19] Over one-third of Croatia's infrastructure was destroyed or damaged – with 100,000 houses and apartments demolished, and large amounts of private property looted.

Other nationalities

Standing aside from the main protagonists in the Yugoslav drama were the country's other nations and minorities. Unlike in pre-1941 Yugoslavia, in Tito's communist state the 'national problem' was no longer a mainly Croat–Serb affair. Tito's federal system gave formal constitutional recognition to the national identity of the Muslims of Bosnia and Hercegovina, the Macedonians and the Montenegrins, as well as upgrading the status of two other national groups, the Albanians of Kosovo and the Hungarians of Vojvodina. In 1990–91 the Bosnian Muslims and the Macedonians sought to play a role in the resolution of the conflict but were sidelined by the main protagonists. Their attempts to secure the retention of a Yugoslav framework, however loose, or – failing that – a civilized parting came to nothing.

The Bosnian Muslims

The two and a half million Muslims (according to preliminary estimates of the March 1991 census), the largest ethnic component of Bosnia and Hercegovina, had backed the latest loose Titoist version of Yugoslavia but were very much against a tightly centralized one under Serbian domination. The Muslim leadership, elected at the multi-party elections in November 1990, in which the Party of Democratic Action captured virtually the entire Muslim vote, expressed itself in favour of a loose confederation of sovereign states like that advocated by Croatia and Slovenia. But this was not acceptable to the more militant Serbs in Bosnia and Hercegovina and the Milosevic regime in Belgrade.

In September 1991 a number of Serb-majority districts in Bosnia and Hercegovina decided to form autonomous regions, analogous to the so-called Krajina in Croatia. In January 1992 they united themselves in a body called 'The Serbian Republic in Bosnia and Hercegovina'. The Muslims saw this as part of the preparations for the creation of a Greater Serbia. Their fear was that this would encourage the Croats in western Hercegovina to start demanding inclusion in Croatia, leading to Bosnia's break-up. To the Muslims, the possibility that the republic might be divided was from the start the ultimate nightmare in which they would be the chief losers – although both the Serbs and the Croats (particularly the Serbs) were also expected to face problems because of the extremely complex ethnic make-up of Bosnia and Hercegovina, which truly resembles a leopard skin.

According to the 1981 census, the Muslims made up 39.5% of the republic's population, followed by the Serbs (32%) and then the Croats (18.4%). In 1981, there were 23 districts in the republic with no absolute majority for any of the three national groups; 32 with an absolute Muslim majority; 31 with an absolute Serb majority; and 14 with an absolute

Croat majority. But in the subsequent decade up to 1991 the national balance in Bosnia and Hercegovina had shifted in the Muslims' favour, chiefly due to their higher-than-average birth-rate. (The Muslim percentage had gone up to 42–43%, according to the provisional 1991 census estimates.) Even so, the Muslims failed to achieve an absolute majority, which would have enabled them to claim the status of a 'republican nation' and Bosnia and Hercegovina as their 'national' state, leaving the Serbs and Croats as minorities rather than equal constituent nations.

The untidy geographic distribution of these national groups had always made the idea of Bosnia's partition an extremely difficult proposition – unless of course it was carried out by force, as in the war now still in progress there. For example, the bulk of Bosnia's Serbs have for centuries been living not in areas contiguous to Serbia but in the west and the north-west of the republic close to Croatia, separated from Serbia by large, mainly Muslim-populated areas in central and eastern Bosnia. Muslims have always been numerically strong in Bosnian regions closest to the Drina river, the historical border between Bosnia and Serbia.

On the other side of the Drina, north-west of Kosovo, there is a strong concentration of Muslims (some 250,000, or about 80% of the total population) in what used to be the Novi Pazar Sandzak region under the Ottoman empire. At the Congress of Berlin in 1878, it was decided that Sandzak (meant to be a buffer between Serbia and Montenegro, the two pro-Russian states) should be garrisoned by Austria-Hungary while remaining under Turkish sovereignty. In 1909, the Austro-Hungarian garrison was withdrawn from Sandzak; in return, Turkey recognized Austria-Hungary's annexation of Bosnia which had taken place the year before. In 1912, during the Balkan states' war against Turkey, Sandzak was captured by Serbia, which subsequently divided it with Montenegro. After 1945 that division was upheld by the Tito regime. The strongest political party in the former Sandzak area now belonging to Serbia is the same party that represents the majority of Muslims in Bosnia – the Party of Democratic Action. The party held a secret referendum in the region on 25–27 October 1991 which resulted in an overwhelming vote in favour of Sandzak's autonomy.

The Croats, most of whom are Roman Catholics, are the most homogeneous element in the republic's population. The bulk of them live in western Hercegovina and north-eastern Bosnia. Both these areas adjoin Croatia and so, in principle at least, it would be easier to hive them off if the whole republic were to be divided. There was a precedent for such a division. In August 1939, under an agreement between the royal government in Belgrade and Vladko Macek, leader of the Croatian Peasant Party (the majority party in Croatia), an autonomous Croatian unit was set up which took in the territory of the post-1945 Croatian republic of the Yugoslav federation plus eastern Srijem (today part of Serbia), the Boka Kotorska district on the Adriatic coast (today part of Montenegro), as well as the predominantly Croat regions of north-eastern Bosnia and western Hercegovina, including the city of Mostar. It had been expected at the time that, under a further reorganization of Yugoslavia, the rest of Bosnia would go to Serbia, but the war intervened in 1941.

Bosnia is an old kingdom whose population consisted partly of Roman Catholics and partly of so-called 'Bosnian Christians' (*krstjani*), a Manichean sect with links to the Albigensians in Italy and southern France. The Catholic church persecuted the Bosnian *krstjani* as heretics. Bosnia fell under the Turks in 1463. Under Ottoman rule, the historic Bosnian lands between the Vrbas and Drina rivers to the east were joined with 'Turkish Croatia' – Croat lands in the west captured by the Turks from Croatia after their conquest of Bosnia proper and made into a large Ottoman Bosnian *pashalik* (province). Many members of the Bosnian nobility (Catholics as well as Bosnian *krstjani*) converted to Islam and were thus allowed to keep their lands. Under Ottoman rule various parts of the Bosnian *pashalik* were settled by mainly Muslim and Orthodox arrivals from other parts of the empire, significantly reducing the proportion of Catholics in the population. This suited the Turkish rulers, who regarded the Catholic church as an ally of its enemies, the Christian princes in the West, and therefore a hostile force.

In 1878, as part of Europe's attempt to cope with the Ottoman empire's slow disintegration, the Congress of Berlin placed Bosnia under Austro-Hungarian administration to deny it to pro-Russian Serbia. Under Austria-Hungary Bosnia was administered as a separate unit detached from both halves of the monarchy. This continued even after 1908 when, to the fury of Serbia and its Russian patron, Bosnia was formally annexed by Austria-Hungary. The assassination by a Serbian terrorist of Archduke Franz Ferdinand, the Habsburg heir to the throne, in Sarajevo, Bosnia's capital, on 28 June 1914 – the anniversary of the battle of Kosovo – was the Serbs' response to Bosnia's annexation.

If the parting among the Yugoslav republics had been a peaceful one, Bosnia's position between Croatia and Serbia could have made it a natural linchpin of a broader regional association. However, this was not to be. In April 1992, on being recognized as a sovereign state, Bosnia became the scene of the next stage of the Yugoslav war, far nastier and bloodier even than that in Croatia which had stopped a few months before, in January.

The Macedonians

Like the Muslims, the Macedonians had a lot to lose from Yugoslavia's break-up. They too saw the idea of a Greater Serbia as a serious threat. It reminded them of the unhappy 1913–41 period when Macedonia was designated as 'Southern Serbia' and the Macedonians were forced to declare themselves as Serbs. But relations with the Serbs had improved in the Tito era and, in any case, Serbia appeared to be engaged elsewhere. And so, ideally, the Macedonians would have preferred to see Yugoslavia evolve into a loose confederation of sovereign states, as advocated particularly by Bosnia but also by some in Croatia and Slovenia. There was broad agreement among the Macedonian political parties about that. Nobody in Macedonia – not even the most fervent nationalists – wanted Yugoslavia to break up. Everybody saw independence as, at best, a mixed blessing.

The reason for hesitation over independence was the Macedonians' fear that a new Albanian entity might emerge from within the old Yugoslav shell, taking in not only the province of Kosovo but also Yugoslavia's other Albanians: those from the districts of Montenegro where the Albanians have a majority, as well as those from the largely Albanian-inhabited western Macedonia, right up to Skopje, the republic's capital. There was some pro-Bulgarian sentiment but it was considerably weaker than before 1914 or 1941. Meanwhile, with all the Yugoslav republics going their separate ways, pro-independence feeling grew in Macedonia too. A plebiscite on sovereignty held in September 1991 showed a majority in favour of independence.

But unlike in Slovenia and Croatia, the Yugoslav army withdrew from Macedonia early in 1992 without a fight. This was a great diplomatic and political success for President Kiro Gligorov, who was, however, helped by the fact that Milosevic and the army chiefs needed their troops for the war then just beginning in Bosnia. Gligorov also scored an important internal political success in managing to persuade representatives of the republic's Albanians to join a coalition government. However, owing to Greek opposition, Macedonia remained isolated; diplomatic recognition was granted to it initially only by a small number of states including Bulgaria, Turkey and Russia. Only after a long interval was it recognized by the European Community and the United States. Throughout the Yugoslav drama Macedonia has remained a second-division player with a vital interest in the outcome, but little direct influence.

The Montenegrins

The same was true, only more so, of the half-million or so Montenegrins, Yugoslavia's smallest nation, which had had a long and colourful history, though always an autonomous one. That autonomy ended in 1918 with a referendum deciding in favour of union with Serbia. Montenegrins supporting union were known as *bjelasi* (the Whites) while those opposed to it were called *zelenasi* (the Greens) – their names deriving from the coloured ballot-slips used in the referendum. The Greens never gave up and some of them plumped in 1941 for the Italian offer of an autonomous Montenegro under an Italian protectorate, while others opted for the Partisans, who offered Montenegro a republic within a Yugoslav federation. After Italy's defeat and surrender in 1943, the Greens faded from the scene, eclipsed by the overwhelming Montenegrin participation on the communist side in Yugoslavia's civil war from 1941 to 1945. But a separate federal republic of Montenegro established under the communists in 1945 represented a victory for the Greens' view that, for all their close historic connections with the Serbs, the Montenegrins are a separate people.

The Greens' long period of dominance in Montenegro's cultural and political life ended with the revolt in January 1989 that brought to power a pro-Milosevic group, an updated version of the old White 'unitarists' who had adopted as their slogan Milosevic's description of Serbia and Montenegro as 'two eyes in one [Serbian] head'.

As in Serbia, the communists emerged as the strongest party in the November 1990 election. But hopes of injections of aid from Belgrade, originally helpful to pro-Milosevic forces, have always been unrealistic and, unsurprisingly, have remained unfulfilled: Serbia itself is in a parlous economic state, aggravated by the huge burden of the financing of the war, first in Croatia and then in Bosnia. Economic sanctions imposed by the United Nations in May 1992 on the rump Yugoslavia as a punishment for its role in the war in Bosnia have also badly hurt the economy. Growing discontent in Montenegro with the republic's role as a satellite of Belgrade has brought the Greens back into the public debate. Montenegro's participation in the war against Croatia proved unpopular, notably in the siege of the historic Croatian city of Dubrovnik on the Adriatic coast; this ended in 1992 with the withdrawal of Serbian and Montenegrin forces to their original positions without any territorial gains for Montenegro. It was interpreted by critics of Montenegro's close Belgrade connection as a national humiliation.

For the time being at least, the pro-Serbian Whites are holding firmly to power, and Montenegro continues to stand alongside Serbia. But tensions continue below the surface. It is quite possible that Montenegro could decide to sever its ever more cumbersome and embarrassing Belgrade connection if Serbia were to become seriously weakened, and seek other partners in the region (Albania, Croatia, Italy). Since Belgrade would not willingly give up its control over Montenegro, whose ports offer its only direct access to the Adriatic Sea, such an attempt could prove extremely costly for the small Montenegrin nation, and this remains very much on the minds of the 'independentists'. That explains why the ever more unpopular status quo in Montenegro is not being challenged more forcefully and why Belgrade retains the upper hand.

The military option

Long before Yugoslavia actually began to disintegrate, there was much speculation in the country as well as abroad about the role the army (sometimes referred to as Yugoslavia's 'seventh republic') might play in a crisis, perhaps working together with the hardliners in the Communist Party. The army conducted a vigorous 'dirty tricks' campaign against the accelerating democratization in Slovenia in the second half of the 1980s, which brought it into open conflict not only with the republic's liberal opposition but also with the then party leadership under Milan Kucan. The generals saw what was happening in Slovenia as a threat not only to Yugoslavia's communist system but also to Yugoslavia itself, and they regarded themselves as the guardians of both. The army had an important stake in the status quo. It was a privileged organization in Yugoslavia, almost a state within a state, regularly spending half or more of the annual federal budget (the equivalent of about 5% of the country's gross national product).

The military leaders showed their commitment to the united communist Yugoslavia by launching a new Communist Party in November 1990 to fight for just such an aim. There was much talk of a possible army-backed coup to overthrow the non-communist governments elected in Croatia and Slovenia earlier that year and to re-create a centralist state that would be federal in name only. General Veljko Kadijevic, the defence minister and by nationality a Serb from Croatia, was particularly exercised by the possibility that 'national armies' in individual republics could eventually supplant the Yugoslav army even if a loose Yugoslav framework of sorts were preserved.

However, attempts between January and March 1991 to stage a country-wide coup came to nothing because of disagreements between General

Kadijevic, a conservative 'constitutional' Titoist, and the more radical (mainly air force) officers. Those in the army who wanted to 'have a go' faced various problems, not the least of which was their realization that to use Yugoslavia's conscript army in such a way would risk its collapse. Although 70% of its officers and non-commissioned officers were Serbs, its recruits were not. For example, according to official figures, nearly 20% of all recruits in 1989–90 were ethnic Albanians. There was a high proportion of Bosnian Muslims, not to mention Croats and Slovenes. Given all those limitations – especially the difficulty of creating enough 'ethnically reliable' units (in other words, units composed of Serbs and Montenegrins) – the army could not hope to gain control over the whole of Yugoslavia quickly, as it might have done in a nationally homogeneous state. In a multinational federation such as Yugoslavia a number of separate coups would probably have been needed to accomplish the task.

In the end, the army failed to produce a Yugoslav version of General Jaruzelski's 1981 military coup in Poland, but events in Slovenia and Croatia presented the army leaders with a challenge they could not duck without a total loss of credibility. Those events also cemented their alliance with Serbia's leader, Slobodan Milosevic. Milosevic had for a long time been trying to mobilize the army for his political purposes but had met with a certain amount of mistrust from the more Titoist generals such as Kadijevic who were keen to preserve Yugoslavia, although not necessarily in order to turn it into a Greater Serbia. In the Milosevic camp, too, there were those for whom the army, despite the predominance of Serbs in the officer corps, was not 'Serbian' enough. However, any doubts were overcome when both sides realized that their interests coincided very closely indeed. What recommended Milosevic to the generals was that he was trying to preserve both Yugoslavia and its old communist regime (albeit perhaps for 'Serbian' reasons). Milosevic was happy enough to concede their Titoism to the generals as long as they were willing to put military muscle into his own power bid. The army rendered Milosevic significant help on the eve of the outbreak of war in March 1991 during large-scale anti-government demonstrations in Belgrade. It sent tanks and armoured vehicles into the streets against the demonstrators.

An irretrievable breakdown

Early in 1991 it began to look as if nothing could keep the Yugoslav federation together any more. With Tito gone, the Communist Party no longer in overall charge and its freed peoples busy quarrelling among themselves, Yugoslavia appeared to have broken down irretrievably. That conclusion seemed to be confirmed by the Croat and Slovene independence declarations issued within a few hours of each other in June 1991. But there were those, in Yugoslavia and – even more – abroad, who hoped that, if there was going to be a Yugoslav separation, it would be both peaceful and temporary. After all, Yugoslavia had been broken up once before – in April 1941 – only to be resurrected by Tito four years later. Besides, historical experience suggested that it usually took a lost war, with enemy occupation thrown in, or some extraordinary natural calamity, for a state to break up completely. In 1991, peace reigned in Europe. The inviolability of European frontiers was anchored in the 1975 Helsinki Final Act. And so, refusing to accept the inevitability of Yugoslavia's break-up and the policy implications that would flow from it, Western governments actively looked for ways of ensuring that the federation survived.

But for the deeply disunited peoples of Yugoslavia to sink their differences and come together again, there would have had to be some overriding new reason, for example the need to avert external danger from a clearly perceived common enemy. But unlike in 1948, when Yugoslavia faced the threat of a Soviet-led invasion, there was in 1991 no external enemy to unite against. It was not the foreign enemy but the enemy (or enemies) within that preoccupied the peoples of Yugoslavia.

Other possible reasons for coming together in a common Yugoslav framework had also disappeared. For example, only a few years before, fear of economic fragmentation and the resulting loss both of markets and of sources of raw materials might have been a strong argument for staying together – even at a political price. But this potentially powerful glue had lost most of its force as a result of the dramatic deterioration of economic relations among Yugoslavia's main republics in the 1980s, with Serbia on one side and Croatia and Slovenia on the other. In most cases, economic hostilities had been initiated by Serbia to put political and economic pressure on the other two, but they in turn had not been slow to fight back.

Indeed, economic factors played an important role in the decision by Serbia and the army to stop those in Croatia and Slovenia from going their own way – by force if necessary. Slovenia's significant income from tourism and industrial exports was an important factor. So were its electronics and engineering factories, particularly in the army's eyes. In Croatia's case, the attraction was its large hard-currency tourist income

(Croatia accounted for 50% of Yugoslavia's total revenue from tourism), as well as its substantial natural gas and oil production (two-thirds of Yugoslavia's total oil output came from the oilfields in northern Croatia), and its rich agricultural lands in eastern Slavonia, in the Croat portion of Srijem and in Baranja. With so many important, apparently irreconcilable interests at stake, it was not surprising that the parting was not amicable. But the decision to resort to force was taken in extremely complex and confusing circumstances that were baffling not only to outsiders but to many insiders as well.

The decision to use force against Slovenia immediately upon its declaration of independence was taken in a political vacuum. The collective presidency of Yugoslavia, which alone had the constitutional authority to issue such an order, was not functioning. This was because Serbia and Montenegro, supported by Kosovo and Vojvodina (by then re-annexed to Serbia and stripped of their former autonomy but still entitled to vote as separate units at the federal level) refused to allow the routine election of Stipe Mesic, a Croat, to a year-long term as chairman of the collective federal presidency in Belgrade. The then federal prime minister, Ante Markovic, had no authority to give such an order. On 21 June the federal government in Belgrade authorized the federal interior ministry to secure the international borders if Slovenia and Croatia declared independence, and asked the army for assistance for its civil authority. Markovic later claimed that the army had exceeded its orders and was acting on its own.

The intervention in Slovenia did not go well for the army. It was both militarily and politically ill-equipped – in contrast to the less well-armed but politically highly motivated and well-organized Slovenes. Not only did the Slovenes fight much better than the army had expected, but the extremely hostile international reaction to the army's intervention surprised the generals and the politicians in Belgrade alike. Intervention in Slovenia was, inconveniently for them, taking place in the full glare of international media coverage, which showed the Slovene David fighting off the Yugoslav Goliath. After three weeks the army withdrew from the conflict, having gratefully accepted the European Community's face-saving peace diplomacy (see Chapter 6). It had in the meantime suffered few casualties but many desertions – among them a number of Serbs.

The war in Croatia, which had already begun before the Yugoslav army had managed to withdraw the bulk of its troops and heavy equipment from Slovenia, was far more prolonged and bloody but also far more successful from the army's point of view. Serb paramilitaries, both locally recruited ones and those trained and armed in Serbia and brought over from there, were used to draw out the poorly-armed and under-equipped Croat National Guard, set up after the proclamation of independence. The army then usually intervened, ostensibly to separate the warring sides and prevent ethnic clashes but in fact to help the Serb paramilitaries consolidate their gains and protect them from Croat counter-attacks. Significantly, there was not a single recorded case of the army training its guns on the Serb forces, whereas there were plenty of interventions against Croat forces. The Croats lacked not only heavy artillery, military aircraft and helicopters but also rifles and ammunition. In contrast, the army trained, fed and supplied the Serb irregulars and provided them with safe communication lines and active protection whenever they came under pressure from Croatian forces.

In the course of the war in Croatia in 1991, the army became a truly Serb force, having lost the conscripts as well as most of the officers from Slovenia and Croatia, together with many from Macedonia and even Bosnia. In Serbia and Montenegro, there was growing resistance against recruitment for the war. In Serbia, an estimated 150,000 refused the call-up and many reservists fled abroad. The army was obliged to fill the gaps by relying more and more on paramilitary groups such as the Serbian Volunteer Guards, the White Eagles and others. The shortage of manpower also led to a growing reliance on artillery and air attacks, which in turn increased the number of civilian casualties as well as the amount of material devastation. By the time the UN-brokered ceasefire came into force in Croatia in January 1992, these combined army/irregular operations in various parts of Croatia had brought under Serb control about a third of the republic's territory, including the bulk of the rich agricultural land and some natural gas and oil deposits in eastern Slavonia, Srijem and Baranja.

The next stage in the military conflict began in Bosnia in 1992. Bosnia was of key importance in the army's eyes. Its central position means that whoever holds Bosnia dominates the whole broader region around it. It was also the main source of troops and arms (under Tito most of the arms factories were situated in Bosnia for security reasons, mainly because of its distance from both the eastern and the western borders of Yugoslavia). The loss of Bosnia could, therefore, not be contemplated by the army leadership. The same was true of the Serbian leadership in Belgrade: in the Greater Serbia project Bosnia was a key element. Military preparations for securing Bosnia were already well under way when the referendum on independence was held on 29 February and 1 March 1992.

The Badinter Commission, which had been looking into the subject of diplomatic recognition of individual Yugoslav republics by the European Community (see Chapter 6), had recommended that such a referendum be held as a precondition for Bosnia's recognition as a sovereign state, which had been requested by the republic's leadership at the end of 1991. Of the 64% of registered voters who took part in the referendum at the end of February 1992, 99% voted for independence, with Bosnia's Croats and Muslims voting solidly in favour. However, most of the republic's Serbs boycotted the referendum at the urging of Radovan Karadzic, leader of the Serbian Democratic Party (SDS) and a close ally of Milosevic. On 6 April the European Community recognized Bosnia; it was followed the day after by the United States. What happened after that was described by the Serbian side as a spontaneous uprising of the Bosnian Serbs (31–33% of the total population) against the threat of Muslim rule over the whole of Bosnia under a fundamentalist Muslim, President Alija Izetbegovic. The record, however, shows that there was nothing spontaneous about the Serbs' actions.

It was, as in Croatia in 1990–91, a carefully prepared and ruthlessly executed plan of territorial conquest carried out jointly by the Yugoslav army and Serb paramilitaries. Planning for it had begun in the autumn of 1991 – months before armed conflict actually started in Bosnia. Artillery positions had been established around major Bosnian cities, including Sarajevo, in the winter of 1991–2. The JNA's units with artillery and heavy armour were transferred into Bosnia early in 1992 from Croatia after the conclusion of the ceasefire there. More came from Macedonia as the army withdrew from there. While multi-ethnic Bosnian territorial forces under the command of the government in Sarajevo were being disarmed, Karadzic's SDS supporters were receiving arms both direct from Serbia and from local JNA commanders.

Serb military preparations were matched by political ones, which culminated in the proclamation of independence of the so-called Bosnian Serb republic (*Republika Srpska*). This took place on 4 April 1992, two days before Bosnia's recognition as a sovereign state by the European Community.

Meanwhile the Serb military preparations had been completed. On 30 March, following a series of deliberately staged incidents in various Bosnian cities (including Sarajevo), General Blagoje Adzic, the JNA's chief, declared that his troops were ready to 'protect' the Serbs of Bosnia. In early April Serb paramilitaries brought over from Serbia by Zeljko Raznjatovic-Arkan, a former bank robber and Yugoslav secret police killer whose force had already committed many atrocities in Croatia, carried out a series of well-publicized massacres in Bijeljina, a town in the predominantly Muslim eastern part of Bosnia close to the Serbian border. This and other raids in the same region led to a mass flight of Muslims. Fighting soon spread to other parts of Bosnia, with the JNA and the paramilitaries trying to secure important communications centres, arms factories and so on – though not with equal success everywhere.

On 14 April President Izetbegovic declared that Bosnia was the subject of external aggression coordinated from Belgrade with Serb SDS leaders in Bosnia. On 27 April he called upon the JNA either to withdraw from Bosnia altogether or to comply with the Bosnian government's request that all the military forces stationed there should be integrated into the Bosnian territorial army. General Zivota Panic, chief of the Yugoslav army's general staff in Belgrade, replied that the army would stay in Bosnia for at least five years. However, on 19 May the JNA command in Belgrade ordered the withdrawal from Bosnia of the personnel who were Serb or Montenegrin citizens. This entirely cosmetic exercise was a politically astute move: some 14,000 army personnel withdrew from Bosnia but about 80,000, with their heavy weapons and equipment, stayed, having been formally transferred to the defence forces of the new Bosnian Serbian republic. They were placed under the command of General Ratko Mladic, who had been commander of the Serb forces in the so-called Krajina during the war in Croatia in 1991. General Mladic's troops quickly surrounded and besieged Sarajevo.

The Serb offensive in the summer and autumn of 1992 led to the capture of about 70% of Bosnia's territory. But it failed in western Hercegovina, where a well-prepared local Croat force under the command of a body called the Croat Defence Council (*Hrvatsko vijece obrane* or HVO), supported by Muslim troops loyal to the Sarajevo government and supplied from Croatia, managed to beat off the combined attack by the army and the Serb paramilitary forces. Some of the military facilities and arms factories in areas of northern Bosnia and western Hercegovina from which Mladic's forces were obliged to withdraw fell into Muslim and Croat hands.

However, the Croat–Muslim alliance did not last long. The Bosnian Muslim leadership's neutrality during the 1991 war in Croatia had angered many Croats both in Bosnia and Croatia and had left a residue of mistrust and resentment towards the Muslims. What these anti-Muslim Croats failed to understand and take into account was the extreme weakness of the Izetbegovic government *vis-à-vis* the heavily armed JNA, now reinforced by the men and weaponry withdrawn from Slovenia and Macedonia and, to a certain extent, Croatia. The Muslims, for their part, were alarmed and upset by reports of talks between Tudjman and Milosevic and their own officials about a division of Bosnia between Croatia and Serbia. News of a plan for a Croat–Serb carve-up of Bosnia gained additional credibility from President Tudjman's oft-repeated preference for a territorial solution along the lines of the 1939 agreement between Zagreb and Belgrade, which had led to the setting up of an autonomous Croat territorial unit taking in a large chunk of Bosnia (including the capital of Hercegovina, Mostar).

There was, therefore, plenty of combustible material lying about waiting to ignite into a full-scale war between the Bosnian Croats and Muslims, who by the end of 1992 found themselves squeezed by the Serb *Blitzkrieg* into less than 30% of the republic's territory – though making up more than two-thirds of its population. Tension between these two groups continued to increase in the second half of 1992 as more and more mainly Muslim refugees, driven out by the Serbs from their homes in eastern and north-western Bosnia, poured into what had been ethnically compact Croat areas in the south of the republic close to the Croatian border.

What sparked off the open Croat–Muslim war in early 1993 was the publication of Western proposals – the so-called Vance-Owen plan, so named after the chief Western negotiators at the time – for Bosnia's division into ten largely ethnic autonomous units or provinces under loose central control from a government in Sarajevo representing the three main groups: the Croats, the Muslims and the Serbs. For a whole year this bitter war took the pressure off the Serb forces led by Radovan Karadzic. Mostar, a beautiful historic city, was the scene of some of the bitterest fighting between the Croats and the Muslims. The Croat–Muslim war ended in early 1994 with near-total defeat for the HVO. The threat of international sanctions stopped Croatia from an open intervention to rescue the HVO.

Meanwhile, under strong American pressure, a ceasefire was arranged; this was followed by an agreement signed in Washington on 18 March 1994 to set up a Croat–Muslim Federation in Bosnia. This was to remain open to the Bosnian Serbs to join – if and when they could be persuaded to do so. Provision was also made for the Federation to establish a confederal relationship with Croatia if both it and Croatia were willing. The possibility of an analogous confederal relationship with Serbia was dangled in front of the Bosnian Serbs, provided they accepted the offer made in the summer of 1994 by the so-called Contact Group of five nations (Britain, France, Germany, Russia and the United States) to divide Bosnia, with 51% of territory going to the Croat–Muslim Federation and 49% to the Serb unit.

The Karadzic regime, however, rejected the offer in August 1994 despite being urged by President Milosevic of Serbia to accept it. Milosevic had been offered suspension of economic sanctions against Serbia if he succeeded in bringing the Karadzic regime round. After Karadzic's rejection of the Contact Group offer, Milosevic broke off political relations with him on the grounds that the Serbs had won all their major objectives and that there was therefore no sense in continuing the war. Belgrade also announced that it was cutting off all aid to the Karadzic regime except for medical and humanitarian supplies, coupling this with the offer to accept international monitors on the Bosnian–Serb border to supervise the Serbs.

The revival of the Croat–Muslim alliance transformed the political and military situation in Bosnia. Instead of facing two adversaries who were destroying each other, the Serbs had to face a much more self-confident Bosnian army, not yet fully integrated with the Croat HVO but cooperating with it tactically in many areas. However, the Croatian Serbs came to the Bosnian Serbs' aid in the late autumn of 1994 in the battle for the Bihac region in north-western Bosnia, strategically important because of its railway linking Knin with Serb-controlled areas of Bosnia. In contrast, the Croat–Muslim alliance came under increasing strain and there was a possibility that the conflict between the two would flare up again. Besides, both (especially the Muslims) lacked the heavy arms with which to defeat the Serbs or at least push them towards significant territorial concessions. By the beginning of 1995 the war in Bosnia had resulted in material devastation and human suffering on a scale not seen since 1945, with more than 200,000 people killed and more than 2 million rendered homeless. Even more than the 1991 war in Croatia, the Bosnian conflict saw massive application of the policy of 'ethnic cleansing' – forcible expulsion of non-Serbs from territories earmarked for Greater Serbia.

Tadeusz Mazowiecki, Poland's former prime minister, appointed in the summer of 1992 by the UN as a special rapporteur on human rights in former Yugoslavia, laid primary blame on the Serbian forces for the atrocities committed in Bosnia – notably the systematic rape of (chiefly Muslim) women and the killing and incarceration of large numbers of civilians in concentration camps in inhuman conditions. According to Mazowiecki's report, all sides in the war had committed atrocities but what marked out the Serb side's was their scale and systematic nature. This led to calls from senior world figures for a Nuremberg-style war crimes tribunal to try those responsible. Those named as prime suspects included the Bosnian Serbs' military commander, General Mladic, Karadzic and Milosevic. The UN Security Council made provision to set up such a tribunal in May 1993; it is now operating at The Hague, with the respected South African judge, Richard Goldstone, as its prosecutor. But the main difficulty the tribunal faces is the refusal both of Serbia and of the Karadzic regime in Bosnia to recognize its authority and to cooperate with it in any way.

By early 1995 the Bosnian war had reached a military stalemate. Nobody had won although clearly the Muslims were the biggest losers, in terms of territorial losses and personal suffering endured. On the other hand, the expansionist Serbian policy had not triumphed: Greater Serbia was as distant and unrealizable an aim as ever, despite the Serbs' vast initial military success. There was a possibility of Bosnia being reconstituted under a form of international tutelage as a single though decentralized unit. But there also remained the possibility of a new conflict in Serbia over Kosovo, which remains firmly in Serbian hands, and in Macedonia, where relations between the country's Slav Macedonian majority and its strong Albanian minority (more than 20%) worsened significantly at the end of 1994 and the beginning of 1995. There was a widespread fear that, in the event of renewed unrest in Kosovo, a campaign of mass expulsion of Albanians from Kosovo could involve not only Albania and Macedonia but also a number of other countries in the neighbourhood in an armed conflict with Serbia. The danger of a wider Balkan war was thus the direct result of the violent implosion in former Yugoslavia in 1991–2.

Given its history, it was not surprising that Yugoslavia should have disintegrated. What was surprising was that it took so many people – including many of those who had been studying Yugoslavia professionally – so long to grasp what was happening and to start thinking of the implications. For there is no doubt that Yugoslavia's disintegration amid a brutal war that has not yet ended – and could even spread – poses serious new challenges not just for its successor states and neighbours but also for the rest of Europe and even the world.

Chapter 6

The external factor

On the face of it, the dismantling in 1989–90 of the external spheres of influence controlling the Balkans* should have been good news for the peoples of the region who had for so long been obliged to toe the line laid down by powerful outsiders. But this new and, for Balkan players, unaccustomed freedom of manoeuvre did not last long. The plague of war in former Yugoslavia, which is far from over yet and may even spread to engulf the whole region, has brought the external powers back to the Balkans with a vengeance. With their Security Council resolutions, arms embargoes, economic sanctions, all manner of diplomatic and humanitarian missions involving thousands of civilians and soldiers alike, they are once again frenetically active there and appear to be getting ever more deeply involved – though, so far anyway, without much visible success. Does this mean, as many people (especially in the Balkans) are saying, that the region once again faces the prospect of being a cockpit of a struggle for spheres of influence? Will the local states once again be actively courted and even bribed by rival external powers engaged in a search for Balkan clients?

Contrary to present appearances, the very opposite may well happen. It is neglect by the outside world – and, therefore, international marginalization – that the Balkan states should prepare themselves for, rather than relentless wooing by potential patrons allowing the locals to play the outsiders off against one another. But why should post-1945 history simply not repeat itself in the Balkans, with the powers doing once again what they did for four and a half decades after 1945 – calling the tune in

---

* Of course, some external influence remains – in Greece, a member of both the EU and Nato, and in Turkey, which, as well as being a Nato member, has become a close ally of the United States, particularly since the Gulf War in 1991.

the region but also reaching deep into their pockets to pay their Balkan pipers?

The answer is that then the Balkans were strategically important – to East and West alike. Today they are not. A clear sign of this was that in the immediate aftermath of the end of the Cold War, with no more East–West competition, interest in the Balkans evaporated. It is true that it has revived somewhat as a result of the war in former Yugoslavia, and even the fear in some quarters of a possible new Muslim state emerging in Bosnia. But overall the world has grown weary of that region and all its problems and so, once the war there is over, with no local riches like oil (except for a small amount in Romania) to tempt outsiders, interest in the Balkans may vanish again. The locals may have to confront, on their own, the daunting task of rebuilding and modernizing their economies and societies. Can they succeed in that task?

Like the rest of the former communist-ruled Eastern Europe, they cannot do it alone and unaided. The political and economic prospects for the ex-communist countries of the Balkans, though perhaps not as bleak as those facing most of the republics of the former Soviet Union, are certainly bleaker than those for Central Europe. Communism had taken deeper roots in the Balkans and had destroyed more of the previous social and economic structures which had, in any case, been far weaker there than, for example, in Central Europe. For a while after 1989 it seemed as if the Balkans might follow the rest of the formerly communist-ruled half of Europe in throwing out communism and all its works quite quickly. In one Balkan country after another the principles and institutions of communism were abandoned and those of political pluralism and the free market adopted.

But it was not long before signs started multiplying that in the Balkans the engine of de-communization was stalling badly. Non-communists are currently in charge in only two of the nine formerly communist-ruled Balkan states: Albania and Croatia. Everywhere else the ex-communists are at the wheel – either alone or sharing the vehicle of state with a co-driver. In some Balkan countries, as indeed throughout Eastern Europe, the ex-communists (or post-communists, as they are increasingly coming to be known) have achieved something they never managed to do during four and a half decades of communist rule: winning electoral victories at the ballot-box at genuine multi-party elections. In some Balkan countries, they never, even temporarily, had to climb out of the driving seat. Serbia and Montenegro have seen no interruption at all to communist power. Slobodan Milosevic, appointed Communist Party leader in Serbia in 1986, won total power there after a purge in 1987, and is still in charge.

The party he heads has changed its name to that of the Socialist Party of Serbia, but that is all. In Macedonia and Slovenia, the ex-communists have also stayed in power but have had to share it with non-communist partners in coalition governments. Romania's governing Party of Social Democracy, though not a direct successor to the old Communist Party, is dominated by the former ruling group of apparatchiks. In Bulgaria the ex-communists returned to power in December 1994 following their outright electoral victory over the non-communist parties.

Thus the break with the region's communist past has nowhere been quick, let alone total, although it has to be said that the ex-communist parties, once back in government, have not tried to turn the clock back fully. All that can be said for the moment is that, while the transition from communism to pluralism and free-marketry in the Balkans has not stopped altogether, it has slowed down to a crawl, with the old communist cadres remaining influential. They owe their comeback at least partly to mistakes made after 1989 by the inexperienced non-communist leaders who had had little or no preparation for power – languishing as they were in prisons or (if they were lucky) in country libraries and statistical offices, while the communists continued to be busy pulling the levers of power. The process of change in the Balkans has been immensely complicated by the war which has affected not only the former Yugoslav republics but the whole region.

Communists and others

Of all the countries in the region, *Slovenia* has made the smoothest progress towards democracy, a free-market economy and the rule of law. It has done so under Milan Kucan, the former Slovene Communist Party leader who used to be on the party's liberal wing and who ushered in the process of liberalization while Slovenia was still part of Yugoslavia. Kucan was re-elected President with a 67% majority in December 1992. Slovenia's Prime Minister, presiding over a coalition government that includes Christian Democrats, is Janez Drnovsek. Like Kucan, he is a former communist, who represented Slovenia in Yugoslavia's last collective federal presidency.

In neighbouring *Croatia*, the ruling party, the Croatian Democratic Union, followed its victory at the first multi-party election in 1990 with successes at the elections in July 1992 and February 1993. During that period it shed from its top echelon most of the former communists it had absorbed in its early days of power. But its leader, President Franjo

Tudjman, who was expelled from the Communist Party of Yugoslavia as far back as 1967, is by inclination no democrat and is displaying strong authoritarian tendencies.

Albania's President, Dr Sali Berisha, at the head of the Democratic Party, defeated the Socialist Party (the renamed communists) at the elections in March 1992 which marked Albania's official break with communism. He is also displaying authoritarian tendencies, but he suffered a setback in 1994 when his draft constitution designed to replace the old, communist one was rejected in a referendum. It may be too soon, however, to see the Socialists benefiting directly from Berisha's mistakes: communist rule had been so harsh in Albania under the notorious Enver Hoxha that it may take his political and ideological descendants a good deal of time and effort to shed his image.

A full-scale communist restoration is not on the cards in any of the south-east European countries. But in *Bulgaria* the old communist apparat has clawed back a lot of its old power (especially in the economy) even though the country has a non-communist President, Zhelyu Zhelyev. It was thanks to the disarray in the non-communist Union of Democratic Forces (UDF) that Lyuben Berov, Bulgaria's non-communist Prime Minister appointed in December 1992, was obliged increasingly to rely for his survival in parliament on the votes of the former communists (now called Socialists) in a tactical alliance with the Movement for Rights and Freedoms, a small ethnic party representing Bulgaria's Turkish minority. This process ended with the Berov government's resignation, its replacement by a brief caretaker administration and eventually the elections in December 1994 at which the Socialists secured a large majority and formed a government under their personable young leader, Zhan Videnov.

In *Romania* President Ion Iliescu, a former member of the old communist power structure and leader of the former communists operating under the name of the Social Democracy Party of Romania (formerly Democratic Front of National Salvation) was re-elected in the second round in October 1992. The coalition regime Iliescu is presiding over is led by a technocrat, Nicolae Vacariou, who is pluralist and reformist in his orientation. However, since August 1994 the government coalition includes the essentially anti-reform, strongly anti-Hungarian Romanian National Unity Party led by Georghe Funar, and since January 1995 the (also anti-reform) extreme nationalist and anti-Semitic Greater Romania Party. In Bulgaria and Romania widespread public disappointment with the meagre and inconclusive economic results achieved in the post-1989 era so far has helped the extremist xenophobic movements directed principally against the local minorities (Hungarians in Romania and Turks in Bulgaria).

As time goes on, the multi-party political system put in place after 1989 will find itself under ever stronger pressure. But the genuinely democratic and pluralist forces in the region have by no means lost the battle. The mistakes and failures of the ex-communists where, as in Bulgaria, they have regained power will provide their rivals with the chance of a comeback. There is some Western business interest in the region: for example, Romania's recently discovered new oil reserves are attracting the attention of Western companies. But foreign investment will be deterred by a combination of continuing instability and the long-term effects of the war in former Yugoslavia (notably UN economic sanctions against Serbia imposed in May 1992, which have made some people extremely rich but impoverished the rest). Such investment is desperately needed to provide a basis for long-term growth but also, in the short term, to kindle just enough hope to enable the countries of the region to maintain social tranquillity and political tolerance during the coming (and most dangerous) phases of the transition process.

Quite clearly, then, the formerly communist-ruled states of the Balkans cannot achieve their political and economic salvation alone and unaided. But who might be willing to lend a helping hand – and purse? For example, what will be the attitude of Russia which has, after the collapse of the Soviet Union, stepped into the shoes of the Balkan states' former neighbourhood superpower and paymaster?

The Russian angle

Even before the Soviet Union's break-up at the end of 1991, the Balkan region had already lost, in the eyes of the leaders in Moscow, much of its earlier strategic and symbolic importance. But, though preoccupied with its own multiple domestic crises, neither the Soviet Union in its last years nor, later on, its successor state, Russia, ever went as far as totally abandoning interest in the Balkans. This was demonstrated in a variety of ways.

Bulgaria
In 1990 the (then still Soviet) government in Moscow resumed, after a short interruption – and on favourable barter terms, too – oil deliveries to Bulgaria, which was strapped for cash and therefore unable to turn elsewhere in search of alternative sources for the energy it had traditionally received from the Soviet Union (see Chapter 4).

There were good economic reasons why Moscow should have wanted to continue to trade (for example, it needed food from Bulgaria), but there was also a political calculation: Bulgaria needed to be stopped from straying uncomfortably far into the Western orbit by associating too closely with the three strongly pro-Western Central European countries, Czechoslovakia, Hungary and Poland. Bulgaria had been trying to join the trilateral cooperation scheme that these three countries had launched in Visegrad in Hungary in February 1991, and had even shown early interest in establishing direct links with Nato. Nato's then Secretary-General, Manfred Wörner, visited Bulgaria in June 1991 at the invitation of the Bulgarian government. None of this amounted to much but Moscow – even in the post-Cold War period – clearly remained hostile to the idea of one of its East European neighbours being linked to Nato. Hence its concern over Bulgaria (even though, of course, the two countries have no common border). Russia has picked up, though in a lower key, where the Soviet Union left off. It continues to single Bulgaria out for special attention, as was shown by President Yeltsin's much-publicized visit to Bulgaria in August 1992, on his return from the economic summit of the Group of Seven (G-7) in London. It was his first visit as President to one of Moscow's former East European dependencies. During that visit a treaty of friendship and cooperation between Bulgaria and Russia was signed.

The Bulgarian ex-communists, in power again after their electoral victory in December 1994, are unlikely to be ready to compromise their country's attempts to move closer to the European Union and to keep on good terms both with Turkey and with the United States by lurching too far too fast in Russia's direction. In any case, there are still on both sides only limited opportunities – except in the crucial field of energy – for an expansion of trade and financial relations. But in the new political circumstances since December 1994, given the Bulgarian Socialists' traditional closeness to Moscow, the Bulgarian–Russian relationship may become more friendly.

Albania

Another sign of Moscow's continuing interest in its former Balkan dependencies was the persistence with which it pressed for the resumption of diplomatic relations with Albania, a country even further removed from its borders than Bulgaria, and the alacrity with which it accepted Albania's offer to resume them in July 1990. Relations with Albania had been frozen since the famous Khrushchev–Hoxha quarrel in 1961. In

May 1991 the Soviet Union sent a large official delegation to Albania to discuss the deepening of political and commercial relations between the two countries. That was, however, the time of growing political and economic chaos in Albania. The reformed (communist) Party of Labour had managed to hang on to power in the first democratic elections in March 1991 but had soon afterwards found itself embroiled in a series of crises. The general strike in May 1991 forced the government's resignation and led to the formation of a national unity coalition, including non-communists. Widespread calls for new elections amid continuing unrest finally resulted in new elections in March 1992 which, as noted above, were won by Berisha's opposition Democratic Party. The new government embarked on a programme of privatization and the construction of a free-market economy for which it secured early and continuous support from the United States as well as Germany and Turkey. There was little in that constellation left for a Russia that had its own pressing problems in the neighbourhood to attend to.

Were the Albanian communists to come back to power sometime in the future, which is not inconceivable, the situation might change – with some scope for a rapprochement between Moscow and Tirana. But even then, given Moscow's closeness to Serbia, Albania's traditional regional adversary, it is unlikely that whoever ruled in Tirana would want to travel too far in Russia's direction as long as it remained friendly towards Belgrade.

Romania

For rather more obvious geopolitical reasons – not least its close interest in the outcome of the political crisis in and around the former Soviet republic of Moldavia (now Moldova) – the Russian government continues to cultivate Romania diligently, just as its Soviet predecessor had done. There is in fact a good deal of continuity in the relationship between Moscow and Bucharest. In April 1991, Romania had surprised the rest of Eastern Europe by the speed with which it agreed to the signing of a new treaty of cooperation, good-neighbourliness and friendship with the Soviet Union, the first East European country to do so since the dramatic changes in 1989.

There was, however, a clear political and economic calculation behind Romania's move: the Soviet Union was a major source of raw materials as well as an important market for the country. Moscow was also seen as a politically significant guarantor of the post-1945 territorial status quo in Transylvania against any future Hungarian claims for the revision of arrangements that had been made under Stalin's personal direction. In that sense, the treaty was also to be seen as a counterweight to Hungary's close and steadily growing links with the West. There was in addition an element of pique: Romania, also anxious to 'join the West', was jealous of Hungary for having stolen a march on it in this area.

The situation has changed quite substantially since then – not only because of the Soviet Union's collapse at the end of 1991 but even more because of closer subsequent Western attention to Romania. At the end of May 1992, the then US Deputy Secretary of State, Lawrence Eagleburger, visited Romania and signed an investment treaty. In the same month the International Monetary Fund agreed a $500m loan. Since then Romania's political and economic contacts with a number of Western states have multiplied. Its newly found oil is obviously an attraction, not least for the countries of the European Union.

On Moldova, which has a 60% ethnic Romanian majority and represents the most significant and potentially explosive issue in Russian–Romanian relations, Romania is performing a careful balancing act. While Russia tries to build a fence around Ukraine by supporting the Russian separatist enclave in Transdniestria, where the Russian 14th Army is situated, the government in Bucharest has reiterated its recognition of Moldova's sovereign borders but has ruled out any unification of Moldova with Romania as well as direct military involvement. Russia appreciates Romania's restraint, which also represents a recognition of most Moldovans' wish to remain independent.

Former Yugoslavia

From the point of view of Russia's vital security and economic interests, the successor states of former Yugoslavia should today be regarded as a region of secondary importance. Yet they remain at the heart of Russia's Balkan policy just as much as when both the old Yugoslavia and the Soviet Union still existed. Today's Russia inherited from the Soviet Union a policy aimed at preserving Yugoslavia. While Mikhail Gorbachev still ruled in the Kremlin, he favoured the forces in Yugoslavia (particularly the Yugoslav People's Army) that were trying to keep the country both socialist and in one piece. This view was shared by the Soviet defence and foreign policy establishments.

In April 1991 General Veljko Kadijevic, the then Yugoslav defence minister, paid a visit to Moscow during which he obtained from the Soviet military leaders promises of new arms and other military equipment. At the same time, the Soviet government promised the army and the Serbian leadership increased oil deliveries. The prospect of continued solid Soviet backing provided important encouragement for the hardliners in Belgrade then preparing for armed conflict in Yugoslavia. In July 1991, after a meeting with Chancellor Helmut Kohl in Kiev, Gorbachev used the outbreak of armed conflict between Slovenia and the Yugoslav People's Army as a lesson and a warning both to Europe and to the Soviet Union that 'what has been built up over many decades by common effort cannot be easily divided' and that 'disintegration cannot be good – it carries with it a huge risk'.[20]

For their part, too, Yugoslavia's hardliners worried, as they were setting out in 1991 to impose their concept of a tighter, more centralized and more Serb-flavoured state on the rest of the population, that the Soviet Union, which they saw as an important backer for their enterprise, might disintegrate. That is why the news in August 1991 of the hardline coup attempt in Moscow was enthusiastically welcomed in Belgrade, both by the Yugoslav generals and by the senior representatives of the Milosevic regime in Serbia. In the same quarters, the coup's failure was seen as a serious setback.

Boris Yeltsin's government has had from the start to cope with the lack of consensus in Russia over what policy to adopt towards former Yugoslavia. The disagreement was part of a wider debate about the direction of Russian foreign policy, in which alleged foreign policy failures were used as a stick to beat the government with on the domestic front. Russia's Foreign Minister, Andrei Kozyrev, then still an apparently firm believer in the 'Atlanticist' line of cooperation with the United States, came under increasingly heavy attack from a coalition of hardline communist and Russian nationalist critics. They charged him and President Yeltsin with failing to come to the aid of Serbia, Russia's traditional ally and also one with a diaspora problem not unlike that of Russia. Those critics contrasted Serbia's policy, which aimed at incorporating all the territories inhabited by Serbs – even where they were a minority – into a Greater Serbia, by force if necessary, with the alleged abandonment to their fate of the 25 million or so ethnic Russians left behind in the non-Russian republics after the break-up of the Soviet Union. This was part of an attack along a broader front which was directed against Kozyrev (as well as Yeltsin) for acquiescing in the bombing of Iraq, a former Soviet ally, and for toning down criticism of Israel's expulsion of Palestinian activists. This was done to please the Americans, said the critics, but had not brought in the expected Western grants and aid.

Western governments, anxious to bolster up the reforming Yeltsin government's domestic standing, tried from the start to involve Russia in the efforts to stop the armed conflict in Yugoslavia and thus to refute the allegations of Yeltsin's critics that Russia was merely the West's 'poodle'. This was difficult as long as the European Community acted alone over the wars in Slovenia and Croatia in the summer and autumn of 1991, but it became easier with the involvement of the United Nations at the end of that year. Once a ceasefire had been concluded in Croatia in January 1992, Russia was invited to contribute a 900-strong battalion to the UN Protection Force (UNPROFOR) being sent to Croatia.

When the war started in Bosnia and Hercegovina, Moscow offered its good offices but left the initiative and the responsibility for the management of the conflict to the United Nations. In the domestic Russian debate, Kozyrev took a stand against the Serbian regime, for which he received much stick from the combined communist-nationalist opposition. Under domestic pressure, Yeltsin departed in January 1993 from the pro-Western course and made several pro-Serb demands. These included the lifting of UN economic sanctions imposed against Serbia and Montenegro – with Russia's concurrence – in May 1992, the prevention of any relaxation of the UN arms embargo on Bosnia, and the introduction of economic sanctions against Croatia after a brief Croat military action in January 1993 against Serb positions in one of the Serb-occupied territories in the south of Croatia near Zadar. After Yeltsin's victory in the April 1993 referendum, Russia briefly returned to a policy of close cooperation with Western Europe and the United States and supported harsher economic sanctions against Serbia and Montenegro, only to revert to a pro-Serb stance once again.

This apparent Russian about-turn had less to do with any traditional feeling for the Serbs as fellow-Slavs and fellow-Orthodox believers than with the Russian *raison d'état*: the desire to preserve some influence in the Balkans and occupy a strong position in the new European security order, and to exploit this position to block as far as possible Nato's involvement in the Yugoslav conflict. The December 1993 election, which resulted in severe losses for the more outspokenly pro-Western forces and dramatic gains both for the communists and for the extremist Liberal Democrats of Vladimir Zhirinovsky, led to the emergence of a strong anti-Nato consensus. In Bosnia, this meant strong Russian opposition to anti-Serb air strikes.

It was the Nato ultimatum to the Serbs in February 1994, issued in the wake of the mortar bomb explosion in the Sarajevo market which killed 65 people and injured more than 200, that gave Russia the opportunity to step in and demonstrate its skill as an operator in the Balkans. General Sir Michael Rose, the UN commander, had managed to persuade the Serbs to agree to a limited withdrawal of their forces before the Nato ultimatum was issued, but then the Russian special envoy, Vitaly Churkin, stepped in claiming credit for defusing a potentially explosive situation by persuading the Serbs to agree to a withdrawal of their forces. Russia also – in a move designed to save the Serbs' face – sent a few hundred extra peacekeepers into Sarajevo. Despite its parlous economic situation, military decline and deep political divisions, Russia thus showed itself capable of pulling off an important diplomatic triumph which, for a while at least, disarmed Yeltsin's critics. But the subsequent fighting around Gorazde which led to a few admittedly feeble Nato 'close air support actions' against the Serbs revealed the limits of Russia's influence: it was able to persuade the Serbs to make concessions only when this helped them save face and avoid being hit by Nato. Equally, Western air strikes against the Serbs at Gorazde, carried out against Russian advice, caused anger and disappointment as well as anti-Yeltsin feeling in Moscow.

A new chance for Russia to adopt, once again, a high profile in former Yugoslavia came with the outbreak of the quarrel in the summer of 1994 between Milosevic and Karadzic over the latter's refusal to accept the peace plan for Bosnia prepared by the five-power Contact Group (see Chapter 5). Like the West, the Russians backed Milosevic and earned warm thanks in Belgrade for pressing on reluctant Western governments Milosevic's demand for a lifting of economic sanctions against Serbia at the same time as or indeed before Serbia's recognition of Croatia and Bosnia. A token of this new closeness between Belgrade and Moscow was a military cooperation agreement, signed in March 1995.

Prospects

Russia's current influence in the Balkans – even in former Yugoslavia – remains limited, compared with that once enjoyed by the Soviet Union. The serious political and economic crisis sparked off by the hugely expensive and humiliating military fiasco in Chechenia in early 1995 has forced the Russian political and military establishment to look inwards. The other preoccupation continues to be the situation along Russia's rim – in the former republics of the Soviet Union which Moscow is trying to reintegrate into its sphere of control, using, in particular, their dependence on Russian energy supplies to enforce its will.

This means that, for the time being at any rate, there are no objective circumstances for an activist Russian Balkan foreign policy – even if an out-and-out nationalist and expansionist post-Yeltsin government should want to embark on one. Russia's continuing financial weakness is perhaps the biggest handicap in this respect. But a basis exists for a restoration of closer relations, especially if things should turn sour between the West and the post-communist Balkan states, forcing the latter to look eastwards. This may already be happening. In its present enfeebled condition, Russia could not overnight fill the gap the West refuses to fill (though the shadowy but rich and powerful Russian mafia, acting in collusion with the reorganized security services, could temporarily step into the breach). But at some stage in the not-too-distant future, a revitalized Russia will probably want to pick up the threads with one or all of its former Balkan allies. Far from being frightened by the prospect of a new closeness with the bear from the east, the Balkan states might actually be glad that someone cares.

The Western stake

Whether or not Russia will, once again, engage itself more actively in the Balkans will depend – quite literally – on the shape it is in and, of course, on the state of its relations with the West. Its continuing close economic dependence on the West seems to rule out, for a while at least, a pre-1914-style Great Power contest in the Balkans, which Russia could ill afford at present. But even if a hardline, neo-imperialist post-Yeltsin Russia of the future did become more assertive in the Balkans, would that matter to the West? If so, what are the real Western interests in the region?

All Western countries, particularly those in Western Europe, would like to see a prosperous, reformed Balkan region as a trading partner. But for the present, unsurprisingly, given the area's political instability, massive trade and balance-of-payments deficits and, of course, the fact that the war in former Yugoslavia is continuing and may even spread, economic interest in the Balkans, particularly by private investors, remains limited.

As far as security aspects are concerned, some Western strategic (if also mostly negative) interests are at stake in the region now. For example, a broader Balkan war involving Greece and Turkey as well as other states would be destabilizing for Europe, the Middle East and even beyond. Nevertheless, was Bismarck right when he said that the Balkans 'were not worth the bones of a single Pomeranian grenadier'? Is this perhaps the time for the West, having discharged its humanitarian obligations in former Yugoslavia, to revert to Bismarckian scepticism and opt for a policy of 'benign neglect' of the region for the rest of this century and beyond?

A tempting thought for Western policy-makers, but also one that, it is to be hoped, will be resisted. The Balkan countries may have lost such strategic and economic importance as they once had, but there are good reasons why they cannot be ignored by neighbouring states or even those farther away. There is also a broader, more positive thought that binds all the specific reasons for continuing to care about the Balkans into one single argument. It is that, for better or worse, in a Europe which has recently seen the end of its post-1945 political division, the cordoning off or 'ghetto-ization' of any of its parts is no longer possible in the longer term and therefore should not even be attempted. Pouring concrete over the dangerously imploding nuclear power station in Chernobyl in 1986 appeared at the time to be an effective way of dealing with that particular crisis. But it is not possible to end the bloodshed in Bosnia or any other troubled corner of Europe by pouring concrete over it – though some hard-pressed Western policy-makers may secretly wish that this were possible.

Moving masses

One of the most obvious ways in which countries pass their troubles on to their neighbours is by sending them their refugees. As the communist system was collapsing throughout Eastern Europe in 1989–90, the region began to figure in public debates in the West as one of the principal up-and-coming problem areas. While it is true that there may have been some tendency to overdramatize the scale of the possible refugee influx caused by the unsettled political and economic conditions in Eastern and Central Europe, few would deny that some of the worst predictions have come true in the Balkans, chiefly as a result of the Yugoslav war.

According to estimates by the UNHCR there were at the end of 1994 some 3.7 million refugees and displaced people on the territory of former Yugoslavia. A large proportion of them depended for their survival on the provision of shelter, food and medicines by outside agencies. The UNHCR also estimated that nearly 600,000 refugees from former Yugo-slavia were scattered throughout Europe. The number of refugees accepted by different countries in Europe varied from 235,000 in Germany to a mere handful in Greece.

Even before the human flood had begun to flow from former Yugosla-via, its neighbours entertained very real fears about the effect large numbers of refugees coming from the east and the south in the near future would have on them.

Austria, Europe's busiest refugee haven for decades, fearing that it might find itself overwhelmed by a huge new wave from Eastern Europe, reinforced security at its borders both with Hungary and with Yugoslavia: the former to stop illegal immigrants from Romania; the latter in response to the war in Slovenia at the end of June 1991. Subsequently, Austria took in, through Slovenia, a large number of refugees from the war in Croatia. But when the war in Bosnia in the summer of 1992 looked like loosing off thousands of westward-travelling (mainly Muslim) civilians fleeing from the horrors of 'ethnic cleansing', Austria imposed severe restrictions on entry, partially in response to a significant rise in xenophobic feeling.

Hungary has had to cope for a number of years with the refugee influx from Romania – both ethnic Hungarians from Transylvania and ethnic Romanians. Its worst fears of a refugee wave from northern Croatia and from Vojvodina, all fleeing from war and prosecution into southern Hungary, materialized in the summer of 1991. In the following months Hungary received and housed, with impressive generosity and little fuss, over 50,000 ethnic Croat and Hungarian refugees, mostly families. It also allowed into the country thousands of Serbs, mainly men of military age fleeing to avoid serving in the war.

Italy, which had been surprised by the arrival of hundreds of Albania's 'boat people' across the narrow Straits of Otranto in 1990–91, feared much larger contingents of refugees from a war-torn Yugoslavia coming either by land through Istria or by boat across the Adriatic. In the event, some came but it was a trickle, not a flood. The war in Slovenia, Italy's immediate neighbour, ended quickly with few refugees. By the time the war had moved to Croatia, there was an independent Slovenia between Italy and Croatia while the Adriatic coast, heavily patrolled by the Yugoslav navy, never became a serious jumping-off point for refugees fleeing to Italy. Croatia took in the bulk of its own – mostly ethnically Croat – population fleeing or expelled from territory occupied by Serbs (nearly 30% of Croatia). It also absorbed the bulk of the Croat and Muslim refugees from Bosnia, although some of the Muslims later moved on to West European and Islamic countries that were ready to receive them. Italy may have accepted few refugees from the war in former Yugoslavia but it has provided generous aid for those quartered in Croatia and Slovenia.

Greece has for some years now been a place of refuge for those escaping from Albania – members of the Greek minority who have been welcome but also a growing number of ethnic Albanians who have not. Some 5,000 of those were rounded up and forcibly repatriated in 1990–91.

More were deported in this manner in 1994. However, the possibility that large numbers of people of all nationalities escaping from the south of former Yugoslavia would arrive in Greece was prevented by the closure of both the borders in the north – with Macedonia and Albania. Greece's past record of assimilating large numbers of refugees is good. In the aftermath of the 1922 war with Turkey in Asia Minor, it absorbed almost 1.3 million refugees, not only from Turkey but also from Russia and Bulgaria. As a result, its total population grew by 25%. The past decade has seen the influx of some 150,000 Pontic Greeks from the former Soviet Union (mainly from Kazakhstan, Georgia, Armenia and Uzbekistan).

The Balkans' potential for creating refugee problems for other countries does not stop there. *Turkey*, thrust by geography into the forefront of the international relief effort in Iraq in the aftermath of the 1990–91 Gulf war, continues to keep a close eye on the situation in Bulgaria for fear of a possible influx of Muslim refugees. In 1989, at the height of the conflict between the then still communist government in Bulgaria and the country's Muslim community, most of whom regard themselves as Turks, no fewer than 350,000 Muslims left for Turkey. The bulk of those refugees have since returned. The present government is striving to ensure greater public tolerance for the Muslims, but some of them may decide to leave again if the situation in Bulgaria deteriorates – whether economically or in terms of human rights. Turkey's current efforts at improving relations with Bulgaria and engaging it in various frameworks of cooperation reflect its anxiety over this issue.

Other, more distant European states have been affected by the latest Balkan convulsions. *Germany* took in a large number of Croatian and Bosnian refugees but internal political upheavals caused by the aftermath of Germany's unification in 1990 led to a wave of anti-foreigner agitation and violence, particularly in eastern *Länder*. Government and opposition parties agreed on a tightening of Germany's liberal political asylum legislation and reductions in the generous welfare provisions. Immigration controls were strengthened in a number of other West European countries, including Britain.

A challenge for Europe

However, refugees are only one – particularly direct and visible – way in which the Balkans have impacted on their neighbours and the rest of Europe. There are others, equally visible and no less important. For example, the war in former Yugoslavia continues to disrupt land and air communications and, therefore, also trade and tourist traffic between Western Europe and Greece and Turkey. In the same way, the protracted economic crisis in the Balkans, aggravated by the war and by the economic sanctions against Serbia, is badly affecting the neighbouring countries. Some individuals and firms have done well – notably those engaged in sanctions-busting – but the general effect on Balkan economies has been little short of disastrous. The war has affected trade, tourism and other activities not only in the frontier regions but also far beyond. Macedonia, land-locked and therefore particularly vulnerable, has been brought to a state of virtual economic collapse. Even Slovenia, out of Yugoslavia and the war since the autumn of 1991, is still affected.

The rest of Europe, particularly Western Europe, could probably continue to get by without paying too much regard to the Balkans, but Central Europe cannot. It has a vital interest in seeing the Balkans restored to some sort of economic and political normality. In fact, what adversely affects Central Europe also has an impact on Western Europe – not only economically but also politically. The West wants the new pluralist, free-market project in the former communist-ruled Europe to succeed. In an increasingly interdependent Europe, that should mean doing something for the Balkans too. But will it be done and, if so, what?

With the exception of former Yugoslavia (which, as we have seen, was a special case), the Balkan countries have always been regarded by the West as a lower priority than Central Europe. The often and openly proclaimed guideline for Western policy on economic aid to Europe's former communist-ruled countries has been for some years that it should be concentrated on the Central European 'hopefuls': the Czech Republic and Slovakia, Hungary and Poland. This is partly because of their direct strategic, political and economic importance to the West but partly also because those states are, in comparison with the Balkan ones, further advanced on the road to the free market and, therefore, better prepared to receive such aid and make good use of it. The scope for other forms of aid to the Balkans, including political and military aid, should in principle be greater, but in practice a similar discrimination operates here too. But that something should be done, within these limitations, for the Balkan states is not in dispute: the question becomes one not of 'if' but of 'who' and 'how'.

Security

As far as the security aspect is concerned, there are not many dilemmas. Nato continues to resist extending a full security guarantee to any part of the former communist-ruled half of Europe, even to the Central Europeans. However, it has had to compromise by, for example, launching the Partnership for Peace (PFP) in January 1994, an open-ended offer of closer political and military cooperation which has been formally taken up by 25 countries (all but three of them either members of the former Warsaw Pact or republics of the former Soviet Union). Ten, so far, have gone one step further, adopting Individual Partnership Programmes specifying the ways in which they would like to work with the Alliance. This scheme includes, from the Balkans, Albania, Bulgaria and Romania.

The United States has, in the aftermath of the Russian intervention in Chechenia, been urging other Nato partners to agree to a process leading to membership for former Warsaw Pact states in Central Europe in the not-too-distant future. But, like its Nato partners, the United States is also anxious not to do anything that would antagonize the Yeltsin government and provide political ammunition for anti-Western and anti-reform forces in Russia. That is why the extension of Nato membership is likely to remain in a state of suspended animation for some time at least.

Nato has become involved in military peacekeeping operations in Bosnia in an uncomfortable partnership with the UN as the latter's sub-contractor. In that role, Nato air patrols have been enforcing the so-called 'no-fly' zone over Bosnia since 1993, carrying out air strikes against the Serbs in Bosnia (and once, also, against a Serb military airfield in Serb-occupied Croatia), dropping food supplies from the air to Muslim enclaves in Bosnia and, jointly with the Western European Union (WEU), patrolling the Adriatic coast since 1992 to monitor the observance of sanctions against Serbia and Montenegro.

The Conference on Security and Cooperation in Europe (CSCE) instituted several changes since the fall of the Berlin Wall in 1989 in order to become a more effective institution with defined competencies and teeth rather than remaining only a forum for dialogue. The CSCE summit in Paris in November 1990 established a Council of Ministers (COM) in Paris with a Committee of Senior Officials (CSO), a subsidiary group at the ambassadorial level. The Paris summit also established three offices that expanded the CSCE security system. A conflict-prevention centre was established in Vienna in January 1991. A secretariat opened in Prague in February 1991 to provide administrative support to other CSCE bodies and information to the public, governments and international institutions. Finally, the Office for Free Elections (OFE) was set up in Warsaw in April 1991 and was expanded in January 1992 into the Office for Democratic Institutions and Human Rights

(ODIHR). Subsequently, the CSCE also decided to appoint a High Commissioner for Minorities. Max van der Stoel, the former foreign minister of the Netherlands, took up this appointment in January 1993. At the December 1994 meeting in Budapest, the CSCE became the OSCE (Organization for Security and Cooperation in Europe) under Hungarian chairmanship until the next plenary meeting.

At the end of June 1991 Austria asked the CSCE (as it then still was) to discuss the situation in Yugoslavia, but insistence by certain countries such as the Soviet Union and Turkey on the maintenance of the unanimity rule, and the need for the government of the country concerned (in this case, Yugoslavia) to give prior agreement to any action taken, left the organization powerless and totally ineffective as a crisis-management body. However, missions from ODIHR did attend the first elections in rump Yugoslavia (Serbia and Montenegro) in May 1992 and advised against international recognition of their results on grounds of electoral fraud. In December 1992, ODIHR again coordinated an international monitoring mission which reported critically on the republican parliamentary and presidential elections in Serbia and Montenegro. But attempts by the CSCE to involve itself in the summer of 1993 in the case of the Serbian opposition leader, Vuk Draskovic, and his wife, Danica, who had been arrested and maltreated by the Milosevic police, were frustrated by the Serbian authorities. Shortly thereafter, the CSCE's long-term missions to the three Serbian provinces of Kosovo, Sandzak and Vojvodina, which had been established in 1992, were expelled and have never been allowed to return. (In December 1993, there was no organized attempt to monitor or observe the latest Serbian parliamentary election, which coincided with the important elections in Russia.)

Political aid
In political terms, the West can provide – and is already providing – considerable help on a bilateral, country-to-country basis to the newly emerging democracies in Eastern and Central Europe in building up their polities. It is easy to be cynical about that effort because it is not expensive to the country providing it, but this does not mean it is not important: quite the reverse. Such political aid, partly governmental but partly also sponsored by political parties and political foundations in the West, has been concentrated on the Central European 'hopefuls', but has recently been given to the Balkan states too, including Albania, where supervision has been an important aid to the democratic process. Britain has taken a leading part in this effort, mainly through the Know-How

Fund operated by the Foreign and Commonwealth Office. Cultural cooperation, including help with education, is also taking place mainly within
the framework of bilateral relations. The more difficult question that
remains is: who will help the Balkan economies?

Economic aid
It is quite clear that the task of economic rehabilitation in the Balkans, let
alone the whole of ex-communist Europe, is beyond any single country's
capacities. The United States, which in 1947-8 extended vital aid to
Greece and Turkey under the Truman Doctrine and supported Yugoslavia after its break with Stalin (as well as setting up the gigantic and
immensely successful Marshall Plan in Western Europe), can no longer
envisage such schemes in these days of large budget deficits. Germany,
a long-established trading partner in the region, as well as in Eastern
Europe, is likely to remain for some time primarily preoccupied with
rehabilitating the former East Germany. Japan, the financial superpower
of the 1990s, could become involved but its geographic distance is an
important deterrent. The Balkans, like the rest of Eastern and Central
Europe, are a job for the multilateral organizations.

Some of them, like the International Monetary Fund and the World
Bank, had already been playing a role in Yugoslavia and, more recently,
have given assistance to Croatia, Macedonia and Slovenia as well as to
Bulgaria and Romania. The London-based European Bank for Reconstruction and Development (EBRD), set up in April 1991 specifically to
help the ex-communist countries of Eastern Europe (with their governments' participation), is playing a distinctive role in assisting with the
direction of investment from the West as well as the development of free-
market institutions and important processes such as privatization.

Clearly the body with the greatest clout is the European Union. It had
had a sort of relationship with communist-ruled Eastern Europe ever since
its recognition by the Soviet Union in the mid-1970s. But it was a distant
relationship, except with Yugoslavia. One obstacle to former communist
countries even applying for membership has always been their lack of
democratic institutions, an essential prerequisite for EU membership.
Another was, of course, that they were not economically prepared for the
replacement of the command economy by the market one.

The Strasbourg-based Council of Europe, a body uniting not only
Nato and EU members but also democratic neutrals in Europe, has been
playing a most valuable role for some years now, acting as an authority
to vet individual countries' democratic credentials while also providing a

lot of help with the process of political democratization and the establishment and strengthening of the rule of law. The need for countries wishing to apply for membership of the European Union to obtain, as a precondition for any application, a 'he-is-a-democrat-and-respecter-of-human-rights' certificate from the Council has been a useful norm for European behaviour and an incentive towards pluralism and human rights observance. The need to reassure the Council encouraged the dismantling of military rule in Turkey. In the 1970s and 1980s the Council's democratic conditionality was seen as a useful way of propelling the then still communist-ruled countries in Europe towards political and economic liberalization.

The sudden collapse of Soviet dominance in Eastern and Central Europe and the subsequent disintegration in rapid succession of Yugoslavia, the Soviet Union and Czechoslovakia, have overwhelmed the Council of Europe, at least in respect of these vetting procedures. However, by early 1995 the Council had accepted into full membership from the Balkans Bulgaria and Slovenia (May 1992) and Romania (October 1993), and applications had been lodged by Albania, Croatia and Macedonia, which enjoy the so-called Special Guest Status with the Council's Parliamentary Assembly, given to all applicant countries (Bosnia and Hercegovina has also been granted the same status but its application for the Council's membership awaits the end of the war). The applicant countries are also signatories of the European Cultural Convention which makes them full partners in about 40% of the Council of Europe's intergovernmental activities. In addition, they have signed a number of other Council of Europe conventions and attend intergovernmental expert committee meetings as observers. Special assistance and cooperation programmes have been established with them to speed up internal reforms, bolster emerging democratic institutions and bring domestic legislation into line with the European Human Rights Convention.

In the immediate aftermath of the collapse of the Berlin Wall in November 1989 and the subsequent changes throughout Eastern Europe, the European Community, too, was suddenly brought face to face with three new sets of problems: first, three credible democratic applicants from Central Europe (Czechoslovakia – as it then still was – plus Hungary and Poland); second, three applicants with less-than-fully convincing credentials from the Balkans (Albania, Bulgaria and Romania); and third, an awkward dilemma over Yugoslavia, a country much supported by the Community but in a state of rapid disintegration and likely to split into several successor states with varying political and economic credentials.

The EC first concluded association agreements, or 'Europe Agreements' with *Czechoslovakia*, *Hungary* and *Poland*, which established free trade between them and the Community. This was done on the grounds that the three countries concerned had made clear progress towards pluralist democracies and market economies. The Central Europeans accepted association but also insist that what they want eventually is full membership. Negotiations, which had started in December 1990, were not successfully completed until 1992. The main difficulties were over sensitive items such as chemicals, steel, textiles and of course Central European agricultural exports to the Community. The compromise solution that was reached was not generous and left the EC's Central European partners disappointed and worried about their future prospects in the Community. (Following the 'velvet divorce' between the Czech Republic and Slovakia on 1 January 1993, the two countries each re-negotiated their association arrangements with the European Union.) Their disappointments with Brussels notwithstanding, the Central Europeans are pressing on with their applications for full membership of the EU.

In the Balkans, *Bulgaria* and *Romania* have concluded Europe Agreements with the European Union: Romania in February 1993, and Bulgaria a month later. Both countries announced that they would, by the end of 1993, initiate a speedy procedure for bringing their statutory legislation in line with EC standards.

In preparation for its Europe Agreement, Bulgaria had concluded a trade and cooperation agreement with the EC as well as joining its PHARE programme. The EC had been charged with the implementation of this programme, launched by the Group of 24 OECD countries (G-24), to help former communist states with the transition to political pluralism and the market economy. Among the areas on which the EC had concentrated its technical and financial assistance were privatization and the restructuring of enterprises, including the modernization of banking and financial services; the promotion of small and medium-sized enterprises and the private sector generally; and labour market agencies and policies, including training. Bulgaria had also been granted unilateral concessions under the Generalized System of Preferences (GSP) and quota liberalization.

The process was even more advanced in Romania, which had opened its contacts with the EC a long time before, while still under the Ceausescu regime, even signing a five-year trade and preferential agreement in 1980. The Community had hoped that giving Romania trade concessions would enable it to withstand politically motivated economic pressures from the Soviet Union. Help was suspended for a while in 1990 because of the post-Ceausescu repression. In January 1991, after both Romania's government and its opposition had submitted evidence about the situation in the country to the European Parliament and to the European Commission in Brussels, the G-24 decided that aid should start to flow. Negotiations for a Europe Agreement also began. Like Bulgaria, Romania also had access to the PHARE programme and the trade and cooperation agreement.

As far as *Albania* is concerned, the EC has taken note of the positive changes that occurred in the political and economic situation in 1991–2. The EC established diplomatic relations with Albania in June 1991 and in July authorized humanitarian aid to the value of 500,000 ecus to alleviate critical shortages. Meanwhile, Albania's leaders started lobbying Western governments for support. Senior politicians visited Britain and Italy in May 1991 with some concrete results: diplomatic relations with Britain and the promise of food aid from Italy. The United States authorized urgent humanitarian aid shipments to Albania after a visit to Tirana in June by the Secretary of State, James Baker. Albania also became eligible for credits from the EBRD.

Albania's 'European destiny' was the central theme of the general election on 22 March 1992 which marked the official end of communism and the one-party state. But the hope raised during the election campaign that political change would automatically open the way for Albanians to work in EC countries to relieve the country's massive unemployment problem was not realized. Negotiations hung fire, leaving Albania still far indeed from its Europe Agreement, let alone full membership of the Community.

Yugoslavia: the EU's biggest challenge

The extremely close relationship between the European Community and former Yugoslavia dates back to 1971, when the government in Belgrade was granted GSP concessions as part of the West's efforts to encourage the Tito regime towards market reforms. The special (and at the time unique) agreement signed as a matter of some political urgency in 1980, at the time of President Tito's last illness, when Western governments seriously feared that Yugoslavia might either disintegrate or return to Moscow's sphere of influence, or both, gave it a large measure of free entry for its industrial products. That was consolidated during the 1980s, the only exception being a few quotas on textile products and restrictions on the tariff-free entry of some other products under the GSP. A special protocol provided Yugoslavia with financial assistance. Under the EC's 1991 batch of policies towards Eastern Europe, Yugoslavia received 30 million ecus within the framework of the PHARE programme: in effect, most of what the Central Europeans were later to get under their Europe Agreements.

By then, however, the main question mark was no longer over the finer technicalities of the next stage of Yugoslavia's relationship with the European Community, but over the future of the state itself. In June 1991, when Croatia and Slovenia declared their independence, they simultaneously announced their intention of eventually joining the EC as sovereign states (until then, Brussels had been working with the republics but always only through the central government in Belgrade). The Community had at regular intervals – notably at the European Council on 28 October 1990 but also subsequently – reiterated its familiar and oft-stated preference for the 'preservation of the unity and territorial integrity of Yugoslavia'. That was the message to all in Yugoslavia from the European Political Cooperation (EPC) meeting on 26 March 1991 which emphasized that a 'united, democratic Yugoslavia' had the best chances of a harmonious integration into the new Europe. Similar statements from the European Community on 9 May and 8 June 1991 also stressed the need for Yugoslavia to stay united.

But then came Slovenia's and Croatia's declaration of independence on 25 June and immediately afterwards the Yugoslav People's Army's attempt to secure Slovenia's borders by force. Those events faced the EC with a challenge to revise its policy towards Yugoslavia. A change in that policy was clearly called for. The 'head-in-the-sand' policy of sticking to Yugoslavia come what might had clearly become inadequate to cope with the new reality. But for the EC, the crisis in Yugoslavia was not only a headache but also an opportunity. The Community was in the middle of a debate about its future development which centred on the subject of a common defence and foreign policy. There was much talk of a common foreign policy but that usually meant in practice that, in the interests of unity, joint foreign policy initiatives were reduced to the lowest common denominator. Yugoslavia offered to Brussels an ideal opportunity to demonstrate that it was capable of having a common foreign policy.

It was in that spirit that Jacques Poos, the Foreign Minister of Luxembourg (which held the presidency of the European Council) declared on 28 June that this was the 'hour of Europe'. The EC entered the Yugoslav crisis formally via the CSCE. The meeting of CSCE Foreign Ministers held in Berlin in June 1991 on the eve of the war in Slovenia had expressed concern about the situation in Yugoslavia. But once war had begun, there was little the organization could do. Its conflict-prevention centre in Vienna had been overtaken by the war. The CSCE's second available instrument, the emergency mechanism, was invoked by Austria and a meeting was held in Prague, a few days after the outbreak of the war. The meeting called for a ceasefire and endorsed a monitoring mission the EC had arranged to send to Yugoslavia.

After thus easing and legitimizing the EC's formal entry into the Yugoslav crisis, the CSCE receded into the background and the Community took the lead. It dispatched, in response to the war in Slovenia, no fewer than three ministerial 'troikas': the first headed by Poos, and then after 1 July (when the Netherlands assumed the Council presidency) by the Dutch Foreign Minister, Hans van den Broek. The ceasefires negotiated by the first two troikas collapsed, but the third, negotiated at talks lasting 16 hours on the island of Brioni, formerly President Tito's residence, came into effect on 7 July and held. In accordance with the agreement between the EC mission and Croat, Slovene and federal Yugoslav leaders, Croatia and Slovenia suspended their independence declarations for three months. The Yugoslav army began to withdraw to its barracks in Slovenia – as did the Slovene territorial forces that had been fighting them. The army was allowed to resume control of the frontier area. The Croat and Slovene parliaments ratified the agreement, which also included provisions for EC monitors to supervise the ceasefire until talks about the future of Yugoslavia began on 1 August.

However, on 18 July the rump collective presidency of Yugoslavia in Belgrade took the decision to withdraw all federal forces from Slovenia, rejecting the army high command's proposal for a total crackdown there. Having lost the political battle in Slovenia, Belgrade decided at least to secure Croatia, with perhaps the option of recapturing Slovenia later. Shortly afterwards the war began in Croatia in the form of attacks by Serb paramilitaries aided by the Yugoslav army, which had gradually emerged as an open protagonist too.

In late July 1991, France raised jointly with Germany the idea of deploying a force between Serbs and Croats in Croatia, within the framework of the Western European Union, a 9-member body which had been dormant since its inception in 1948 but which had become more important in the late 1980s because many saw it as a possible defence arm for the EC. The French initiative came to nothing, but in September 1991, as fighting in Croatia continued with ceasefire after ceasefire breaking down, the possibility of sending troops from the EC member states wearing WEU hats into Yugoslavia was raised again. The renewed French proposal was supported by Germany, Holland and Italy, but opposed by Britain. The non-interventionists were helped by two factors: the (entirely predictable) absence of an invitation for a WEU force from Serbia, and the British determination to nip in the bud a Franco-German idea for a Euro-army to which Britain would probably end up being the main contributor. Here, as on many subsequent occasions, the more immediate political concerns of the EC member states squeezed the situation on the ground in Yugoslavia lower down the agenda.

Having failed to stop armed conflict in Yugoslavia, the EC was reduced to managing it. This happened in two ways: through continuing to arrange ceasefires on the ground and through the peace conference on Yugoslavia at The Hague. Both efforts failed. The only ceasefire successfully brokered by the beginning of 1992 was that by Cyrus Vance, a former US Secretary of State, on behalf of the UN. The peace conference, hurriedly convened in September 1991 by Lord Carrington, the former British foreign secretary who had negotiated the end of the war and the political settlement in Zimbabwe/Rhodesia in 1979, proved to be little more than a talking shop. It brought together the Yugoslav federal presidency, the federal government and the presidents of the six republics, but when Lord Carrington suggested the establishment of sovereign and independent republics for those who wished it, Serbia rejected his proposal. The conference collapsed in November 1991 and the UN was brought in.

By then, an arbitration commission, set up with a French constitutional lawyer, Judge Robert Badinter, at its head, had reported back. Its main conclusions were that Yugoslavia was in 'a state of dissolution'; that self-determination must not involve changes to existing republican borders at the time of independence (except when the parties concerned agreed otherwise); and that Croatia, Macedonia and Slovenia should be given diplomatic recognition (in Croatia's case, following changes in constitutional arrangements to protect the position of Croatia's Serb minority). Bosnia could also be recognized if the majority of its population voted for independence at a referendum. The EC decided in December 1991, after a long and acrimonious debate, to recognize Croatia and Slovenia, but by then the main role in handling the settlement of the conflict in Croatia had, at the EC's request, passed to the UN, which arranged in January 1992 for four Croatian regions that had come under Serbian control during the war to be placed under the protection of UNPROFOR pending the final political solution. The row in the EC was between pro-recognition Germans, acting under pressure from their public opinion to do something to stop the war in Croatia, and the anti-recognition British and French, who were looking for an overall settlement that might keep Yugoslavia together, and who were afraid that early recognition of those two republics would prejudice such a solution. The Germans prevailed, but their diplomatic victory soured relations within the Community.

In deference to Greece's objections, Macedonia remained unrecognized, but Bosnia was accorded recognition by the EC on 6 April 1992, a month after its referendum. It was subsequently recognized also by the United States and received into the United Nations – together with Croatia and Slovenia – on 22 May. As already described in Chapter 5, the war in Bosnia, which had been started by the Serbs even before Bosnia's formal diplomatic recognition, led to UN-imposed economic sanctions against Serbia. Calls by the government in Sarajevo for international military intervention to defend Bosnia against Serbia's aggression were rejected, but a large-scale humanitarian effort was mounted under the protection of UN forces. Joint diplomacy resulted in an EC–UN conference in London in August 1992, which was also attended by the permanent members of the UN Security Council and by representatives of the G-7 and of the non-aligned nations. Since Lord Carrington had resigned, Lord Owen, another former British foreign secretary, was appointed co-chairman with Cyrus Vance of a new peace initiative based in Geneva. As described in Chapter 5, the Vance–Owen plan was rejected in April 1993 by the Bosnian Serbs, as was, a year later, the Contact Group plan.

Following the US Democratic Party's victory at the November 1992 presidential election, the United States became more actively involved in various diplomatic efforts aimed at solving the crisis in former Yugoslavia. However, American reluctance to commit troops to peacekeeping operations on the ground in Bosnia and Croatia while calling for more energetic action to punish the Serbs and help the Bosnian Muslims by, for example, lifting the UN arms embargo for Bosnia, led to bitter recriminations within the Western camp. Britain and France objected that American proposals were endangering the UN forces' mission, to which the British and the French were the main contributors. American diplomacy, however, achieved a significant breakthrough in early 1994 by brokering a ceasefire in a bitter armed conflict between the Bosnian Croats and Muslims which had started a year before. The ceasefire agreement was accompanied by one setting up a Bosnian Croat–Muslim Federation. The European Union, for its part, undertook in 1994 the task

of rebuilding the city of Mostar, where the bitterest Croat–Muslim fighting had taken place in 1993; the EU's own administration there was
presided over by Hans Koschnick, a German Social Democratic politician and former Mayor of Bremen.

In early 1995 a military stalemate of sorts seemed to be emerging very
slowly in Bosnia but with no early prospect of a political settlement
either there or in Croatia. Meanwhile both the EU and the UN were trying
to devise ways of preventing the war spreading to other parts of former
Yugoslavia.

Chapter 7

A new Balkanscape

Friends and neighbours

Rescue for the hard-pressed Balkans should be both a long-term and a short-term attempt. As Western governments and institutions cope with the immediate challenge of the war and its long-term consequences, an important role in the short-term salvation of the Balkans is being played by countries like Austria, Italy, Turkey and other neighbours. They qualify for the task by virtue of both their geographical proximity and their economic and security interests in the area. Dealing with the biggest problem in the Balkans today – Yugoslavia's break-up – will, however, involve all of its neighbours, the better-off ones as well as those which are themselves in need of assistance.

Fortunately, unlike in the pre-1941 period, there are at the moment no vultures perched on former Yugoslavia's borders, waiting to pounce on the former federation's corpse to grab their pound of flesh. A more apt image to describe Yugoslavia's neighbours is that of worried tenants in an apartment house who have already lost a lot of sleep because of a 'mother of all rows' at one of the apartments, threatening to spill over onto the landings and staircases. Humanity but also self-interest inspires them to offer cups of tea, or possibly something stronger, to the inhabitants of the disturbed apartment. Outlines of this good-neighbourly activity, which also allows glimpses of possible new future Balkan alliances, are slowly becoming visible.

Austria
Austria, for which the old Habsburg connection as well as geographical proximity are important factors, showed the greatest readiness to help

Croatia and Slovenia as they were disengaging from Yugoslavia. Even before the war in Slovenia, Austria had allowed discussions about linking the Austrian schilling with the new Slovene and Croat currencies that would replace the Yugoslav dinar after independence. The generous moral support to Slovenia in its war with the Yugoslav army by both the Austrian government and its people has created a new bond between two peoples who had long been viewing each other with mistrust. Austria extended full moral, political and humanitarian support to Croatia during its desperate struggle for survival in the summer and autumn of 1991, but its involvement in political and humanitarian aid for Bosnia was tempered by the need to appease pressures to limit the influx of refugees from the war-torn Balkans region into Austria. A particularly important role was played in all those Austrian efforts by its then Foreign Minister, Alois Mock.

It is already clear that Austria intends to use its membership of the European Union to promote, within the limits imposed on all members by the discipline of EU's common foreign and security policy, closer links between the Union on one side and Croatia and Slovenia on the other. In the case of both republics this should lead to full EU membership, but with the proviso that Croatia will have to await the end of the war in Bosnia and its political arrangement with its Serb minority. Austria has accepted its role as a 'minder' for those two aspirants. Meanwhile, a connection that has opened up new trading and other opportunities cannot do Austria any harm. The economic motive behind Austria's *Südostpolitik* is clearly visible in the cooperation its *Länder* have been pursuing since 1978 with Croatia, Slovenia and other members of the Alpen-Adria regional 'working community'.

Hungary

Like former Yugoslavia's other neighbours, Hungary faces special dilemmas, connected with its concern for its minorities abroad, in responding to the new reality developing on the ruins of Tito's Yugoslavia. For decades, Hungary had regarded the Yugoslav federal framework as satisfactory for the country's Hungarian minority, nearly half-a-million strong and mainly situated in Vojvodina. Until the late 1980s, the treatment of the Hungarian minority in Yugoslavia was far more liberal than in Romania or Czechoslovakia. The fear in Budapest was that, in a Vojvodina that was part of an independent, strongly nationalistic Serbia, the Hungarian minority's position would become dangerously exposed. Hungary, realizing that it had no power to influence the deteriorating situation in Yugoslavia, followed a double strategy.

On the one hand, it tried to keep at least on speaking terms with Serbia. That proved extremely difficult, especially as there had been growing Serbian nationalistic pressure on the Vojvodina Hungarians since the pro-Milosevic regime came to power in the province in the autumn of 1988. In 1991–2 the notorious policy of 'ethnic cleansing' came to be applied also to the Hungarians in Vojvodina and in the Serb-controlled regions of Eastern Croatia. The Hungarian government's protests in Belgrade and interventions at international level had no effect.

In contrast, Hungary's already close relations with Slovenia and Croatia continued to develop apace. The sale of light arms in the autumn of 1990 to the Croat government for its new gendarmerie exposed the Budapest government to accusations from Serbia of interference in Yugoslavia's domestic affairs. Hungary's domestic opposition also tried to exploit the episode to attack the coalition government, in which the Hungarian Democratic Forum (HDF) was the main element. Ideological closeness helped foster good relations with Slovenia and Croatia, both of which elected in the spring of 1990 reformist governments similar in outlook to that led by the HDF.

Ideology may no longer be a bond since the defeat of the HDF-led coalition in May 1994 and the advent to power of a coalition led by the former communists under Gyula Horn as prime minister. However, like Austria, land-locked Hungary has a strong economic interest in developing closer links with both Croatia and Slovenia. One important element of that cooperation could be a new highway planned to link Central Europe with Trieste via Slovenia. The other is the so-called Adria pipeline, which dates back to the era of cheap oil before 1973. Cut by the Serb occupation of a southern Croat region through which it passes, the pipeline has become topical again because of the agreement reached by Zagreb and the rebel Serbs late in 1994 to reopen it. This is of some considerable interest to Hungary which needs to diversify its oil imports in view of the reduced Soviet deliveries to Central Europe. Adriatic ports are also of interest, notably the big port of Rijeka in Croatia, familiar (under its other name, Fiume) to the Hungarians from the pre-1918 period as an important trade outlet.

Italy

As the Yugoslav crisis erupted in 1990–91, Italy's then Socialist foreign minister, Gianni de Michelis, produced a number of schemes, in each of which a united Yugoslavia formed a key element. That was not accidental: de Michelis had been a strong supporter of Yugoslavia in public as well as an influential voice in its favour behind the scenes in EC councils. Italy's support for Yugoslavia was based on the perception (derived from historical experience) that it was easier to do business with – and obtain concessions from – a government in Belgrade than those in Zagreb and Ljubljana. It was of course easier, when it came to accommodating Italy's aspirations and interests in the Adriatic region, for the more distant (and therefore also more relaxed) Serbs to be cooperative than for the Croats and the Slovenes, who are right next door to Italy and ready to defend every inch of their coast and every island, however small.

Another factor in Italy's thinking about Yugoslavia's dissolution was the possibility that it might set a precedent for and encourage demands by the German-speaking population in Alto Adige/South Tyrol to rejoin Austria. And finally, as already indicated, Italy feared a large refugee influx from a Yugoslavia breaking up amid disorder and civil war. Those fears had been reinforced by the Albanian exodus to Italy in 1990-91. But, like the other governments of the region, Italy in the end took a pragmatic view of the Yugoslav situation and, once disintegration had become unstoppable, found no difficulty in agreeing with Germany that diplomatic recognition should be extended to Croatia and Slovenia. For its part, it lost no time in developing close political and commercial contacts, through the consulates it already had in Zagreb and Ljubljana, with the governments of those two former republics. That cooperation had a solid foundation in unspectacular but useful exchanges they had had over a number of years with four northern Italian regions within the framework of the Alpen-Adria 'working community'.

A more ambitious, chiefly Italian, project for the region was the so-called *Pentagonale* grouping. That was launched first in 1989 as the *Quadrilaterale*, and included Austria, Hungary, Italy and Yugoslavia; Czechoslovakia was a later addition. Poland joined in July 1991, making it the *Hexagonale*. Politically, it was a bid by the Italians for leadership of Central Europe; behind it lay their old fears of German dominance both in Central and in Southern Europe. Austria welcomed the *Pentagonale* as an extension of the good work begun by the more modest Alpen-Adria grouping, and as a useful link with Czechoslovakia. The Czechoslovak President, Vaclav Havel, showed a keen personal interest in the political aspects of this plan, whereas Hungary and Yugoslavia had been chiefly interested in the possibilities the framework seemed to offer for the regional infrastructure, especially in transport and energy. The group eventually developed into a body called the *Central European Initiative*, with Croatia and Slovenia replacing Yugoslavia and the Czech and Slovak

119

Republics taking the place previously occupied by Czechoslovakia.

In April 1991 Italy launched another regional plan for a Mediterranean regional community to include Italy's southern regions, Albania, Greece, Serbia, Montenegro, Croatia and – as an observer – Slovenia. The aim of the scheme was cooperation in the northern Mediterranean to ensure greater regional stability, a key Italian concern. Little has since been heard of this plan, but it may well come to be revived because it would provide a useful framework for Italy to help Albania and Montenegro in the economic field. It could also one day help bring Serbia out of its present isolation.

Italy's relationship with Croatia and Slovenia deteriorated in 1994. The cause was the advent to power in Italy of a coalition, with the National Alliance (*Alleanza Nazionale*), a direct offshoot of the former neo-Fascist Italian Social Movement (*Movimente Sociale Italiano* or MSI) as one of the three partners. The new government, presided over by Silvio Berlusconi, vetoed for more than a year – right up to March 1995 – the start of EU talks with Slovenia over the question of Union membership. While AN leaders talked in general terms of the need to renegotiate the 1975 Osimo Treaty between Italy and the then Yugoslavia which had regulated all outstanding territorial and other questions between the two states, Italy asked Slovenia at bilateral talks to adapt its property law in line with provisions of an EU Association Agreement, which would have allowed the Italians to buy up the houses and lands of Italians who left or were expelled after 1945. These developments created an atmosphere of unease also in Croatia, which braced itself for a possible renewal of Mussolini's old aspirations to Croatia's Adriatic coast.

Romania

Romania had shown a keen interest in developing close relations with Serbia. This was partly a reflection of strong common economic interests (hydroelectric power stations on the Danube, cooperation in arms production with the Yugoslav army, and other joint projects); and partly, too, a reflection of the ideological closeness between Ion Iliescu and Slobodan Milosevic, both populist communist leaders.

The fact that both Serbia and Romania have sizeable and vocal Hungarian minorities – though Romania's is much larger than Serbia's – was also a common bond. Romania found itself in international isolation in 1990–91 as a result both of its reluctance to reform and of its repressive policy towards its Hungarian minority. It appreciated close relations with Serbia, which had also provoked international criticism first by its repressive policy towards the Albanians in Kosovo and the Hungarians in Vojvodina and later an even stronger world condemnation for its role in instigating the wars in Slovenia, Croatia and Bosnia. Romania and Serbia share enough old traditions and present interests to ensure that a close relationship between the two states will endure. Although the friendship with Serbia has helped to lessen Romania's sense of international isolation, that isolation has never been absolute: outside the Balkans, Romania enjoys some backing from the Latin bloc in Europe – France, Italy and Spain.

Greece
Greece has a close interest in the fate of its national minority in southern Albania but no official territorial claims there. However, there are irredentist figures in Greece such as Archbishop Sevastianos in Konitsa in Epirus, a supporter of the so-called Movement for the Recovery of Vorio Epirus, who is campaigning for the implementation of the 1914 Protocol of Corfu, which gave northern Epirus to Greece but which was revoked by the 1921 Ambassadors' Conference. This sort of talk gives the Albanians at least some grounds for believing that, if serious civil disorder occurred in Albania, Greece might be interested in the dismemberment of their country.

Some of Greece's worries about the break-up of Yugoslavia were grounded in practical considerations such as the threat that war in Yugoslavia posed to Greece's commercially important transit routes through that country. Even more important, Greece was hostile towards the prospect of an independent Macedonia under a nationalist government with a mission to unite all Macedonians – including those in Greece whose existence Greece denies, as well as those in Bulgaria whose existence Bulgaria denies. It should not be forgotten that the ruinous civil war in the late 1940s and early 1950s had been waged by the Greek communists from bases in Yugoslav Macedonia and that the insurgent Greek communist units of General Markos had contained a large number of Greek citizens regarding themselves as ethnic Macedonians. After their defeat, many of these 'Slavophones' (Greek Macedonians) were obliged to take refuge in various East European countries. This was one of the factors that helped to reduce the Slav minority in Greece, already diminished by the voluntary exchange of populations with Bulgaria under the Treaty of Neuilly in 1919.

Greece's common front with Bulgaria over Macedonia was manifested during a visit to Athens in March 1991 by the then Bulgarian

Prime Minister, Dimitar Popov, when he and the Greek Prime Minister, Constantine Mitsotakis, issued a statement denying the existence of ethnic minorities on their respective territories. But Greece was deeply upset when Bulgaria, making a big break with the past and – more immediately – fearing that Serbia might make a grab for Macedonia with support from the Greeks, recognized Macedonia in January 1992 and brought Russia in tow. Greece was also upset by the improvement in relations between Bulgaria and Turkey, which had recognized Macedonia promptly. However, Greece was reassured by Milosevic's visit in April 1991; he was treated by the conservative Greek government as a head of state, and this confirmed the widespread impression that Greece could rely on Serbia as a valuable ally over Macedonia. Greece appreciates the fact that Serbia has so far shown no inclination to recognize the government in Skopje and has not opposed Greece's trade and transport boycott of Macedonia, which has been in operation since February 1994. In return, Greece (together with Cyprus) has provided Serbia with invaluable, if indirect, assistance in sanctions-busting.

For Greece, even more pressing than its security concerns in the western Balkans is its troubled unequal relationship with its fellow-member in Nato, Turkey, which many Greeks claim to see as a modern version of the Ottoman empire about to embark on another conquest of the Balkans. Several disputes, including that over Cyprus, divide Greece and Turkey, but behind it all lies the Greeks' awareness of their country's weakness in relation to the 'colossus on the Bosporus'.

Both Greece and Bulgaria see Turkey as a potential threat. In addition, both have Muslim minorities which they fear Turkey may increasingly want to take under its wing. Both these factors help account for the close relationship between the two countries that began in the late 1960s while Bulgaria was still under the communists and Greece under the colonels, and that has developed over the years. Greece gave Bulgaria some food aid during the difficult 1990–91 winter, including a gift of 15,000 tons of oranges and other citrus fruit in January 1991. But Greece has some real economic interests in Bulgaria and since the start of the Yugoslav war it has relied on transport routes through Bulgaria and then directly through northern Serbia into Hungary. Bulgaria had hoped that Greece would speak up for it in the European Community and generally help it with credits and private investment. These hopes have been disappointed and Bulgaria has lately been increasingly looking to Turkey for investment and trade, though it has not totally given up the Greek economic option.

Bulgaria

It is important for Bulgaria to maintain, for the foreseeable future, its trade with Russia, Ukraine, Belarus and other Soviet successor states. Russia supplies the bulk of its energy requirements. Given its current desperate straits, sheer economic survival is the principal preoccupation of Bulgaria, both government and people. But the Bulgarians were anything but pleased at the prospect of Yugoslavia breaking up in 1990. The idea of Macedonia, for decades the cherished national goal, becoming detached from Yugoslavia and, in principle at least, free to join Bulgaria, evoked not joy but anxiety, particularly among politicians. In their eyes (though they could not admit it in public) the impoverished Macedonia, with its large Albanian population, did not look like a desirable acquisition but rather a headache to be shared – with Greece, in the first place, which was similarly dismayed by the unfolding of events in Yugoslavia.

The Bulgarians reckoned (correctly) that Greece would not look kindly upon Macedonia's union with their country. Bulgaria could not, in any case, afford to quarrel with Greece or cross it. For one thing, as just indicated, the Bulgarians hoped Greece would plead their case over EU membership. Moreover, in security terms, the Greek connection was a safeguard for Bulgaria against possible intervention by Turkey.

Given those problems (and Bulgaria's fear that Serbia might try to grab Macedonia), an acceptable solution of this question, from the Bulgarian point of view, could be an independent Macedonia under a leadership ready to accept as final its borders as they were within Yugoslavia, to renounce any territorial aspirations towards either Bulgaria or Greece, and to promise not to act as a protector for any Macedonians living in those two states. At present, Macedonia's future as a state appears stable, especially from the diplomatic point of view, though internally it remains fragile owing to the continuing tension between its Macedonian majority and its large Albanian minority. However, if an independent Macedonia on its own did not prove ultimately to be a viable state, its most likely final home could, after all, be Bulgaria. But this would represent a stable solution only if it were approved by a referendum of the Macedonian and Bulgarian peoples and within a broader Balkan consensus. In other words, it would need the (unlikely) consent of Bulgaria's neighbours, Greece and Serbia, as well as Albania. In view of that, the future of Macedonia remains uncertain.

Albania

Contrary to frequent Yugoslav accusations of interference, communist Albania never actively encouraged secession in the Kosovo province. Moreover, it has given only verbal support to the Kosovo Albanians' unsuccessful demand for greater autonomy (as in their 1981 demonstrations for a republic within Yugoslavia on a par with Serbia, Croatia and the others). Clearly, power was always more important to Enver Hoxha than a foreign policy adventure likely to provoke not only armed conflict with a stronger (and internationally popular) neighbour but also possible internal turmoil in Albania itself, which might endanger his position. Persistent claims by Belgrade of 'Tirana-inspired irredentism' never had any substance to them and were meant for domestic consumption.

But the political upheaval in Albania during 1990–92 that led eventually to increased foreign contacts have all had important consequences for the situation in Kosovo too. There have been contacts between Kosovo's ethnic Albanian politicians and both the opposition and the government in Tirana. Significantly, for the first time the government in Tirana is under pressure to do more for its fellow-Albanians than complain about their oppression in Serbia. But its difficulty is to know exactly what to do without encouraging a dangerous general uprising, which might be followed by a savage campaign of 'ethnic cleansing' resulting in a mass exodus of ethnic Albanians from Kosovo into Albania and the parts of Macedonia inhabited by Albanians. That would pose difficult dilemmas that the hard-pressed Berisha regime in Tirana would rather not face but may not be able to duck.

History marches on. The combination of the political opening in Albania and the closing-off of the recent Albanian hopes of autonomy in Yugoslavia has united the Albanians in Albania and those outside its borders. The situation in former Yugoslavia means that the prospect of a Greater Albania has become a possibility for the first time since 1945 – although this does not mean it is likely, at least for a long time: much would still have to change in the immediate neighbourhood, and within Albania itself. Ironically, one of the most significant single factors that has helped to make the prospect real, at least in the longer term, has been the Greater Serbian (and strongly anti-Albanian) offensive under Milosevic. This has destroyed the Yugoslav state and at the same time united Kosovo's Albanians in opposition to it and made them incline towards union with Albania. A strong, cohesive Yugoslavia could have continued to hang on to Kosovo indefinitely. Serbia's attempt to do so will ultimately fail. Kosovo's independence seems inevitable, although it will not happen without a struggle with Serbia, possibly even a pre-emptive Serbian strike against a still rather weak Albania; or, at least, a division of Kosovo by Serbia, resulting in the local majority Albanian population being squeezed into a small, poor section of the province, with Serbia retaining the mines, the factories and the best land. Kosovo's union with Albania seems a more distant prospect.

Networks for the new millennium

Regional groupings are likely to assume an ever greater importance in the Balkans – even if not immediately. Looking beyond the present distressing war in former Yugoslavia, and the eventual ebbing away of the tide of Serbian expansionism, it is possible to discern the shape of two such groupings in south-eastern Europe, each bound together by a combination of tradition and common economic and security interests, but also with links to others in the neighbourhood and within the broader European context. These groupings will comprise sovereign states coming together not to build Berlin or Chinese walls to keep others out, but to forge links to neighbours and others beyond in customs unions, free-trade areas and so on. One of the functions of powerful outsiders could be to foster this openness and discourage inward-looking tendencies.

In the west could be a loose grouping of (mainly) Catholic states, those which had once been part of the Habsburg empire – a *Kleinmitteleuropa* (Little Central Europe) bound together by tradition but, even more, by perceived common economic and security interests and linked (together or separately) to other states and groupings, including the European Union. Its members could be Austria, Bosnia (a Habsburg land between 1878 and 1918), Croatia, Hungary, Slovenia and Slovakia. This grouping could be loosely linked with the Czech Republic, Poland and the Baltic states in the north, Ukraine in the east, and Italy in the south-west.

To the east could be a loose grouping of states – call it a Balkan confederation, or perhaps *Balkania* – sharing the Orthodox tradition and cooperating in the economic and security fields (here, in particular, the Balkan cooperation machinery set up at the 1988 Balkan states conference and pushed aside since then could be dusted off and further developed). This grouping could include Bulgaria, Greece, Romania and Serbia, with Macedonia in the middle as an independent buffer state or perhaps, ultimately, a part of Bulgaria – should Greece and Serbia permit and the Macedonians despair of a future on their own.

Alternatively, there could be two groupings: one made up of Greece,

Romania and Serbia (with Cyprus at the southern end) and the other consisting of Albania and Montenegro looking towards Italy for support. Such an arrangement offering individual states additional security could perhaps provide a framework for a gradual solution – or at least for a defusing – of the explosive Kosovo issue that divides Serbia and Albania. But Kosovo represents perhaps the knottiest problem in the whole of the Balkans today and may be incapable of resolution without a further war.

Turkey, despite its traditional caution, could eventually lead, within a 'Black Sea Cooperation Zone', the grouping that included Azerbaijan, Bulgaria, Georgia, Moldova, Romania, Ukraine and even Russia. In the Balkans, Turkish backing for Albania would help to deter those in Greece and Serbia who may still be dreaming of carving up Albania between them. The same is true of Macedonia. But Turkey's involvement in the Balkans, however modest so far and closely coordinated with the United States, evokes unease in the region not just because of the memories of Ottoman rule but also because of the so-called 'Islamic dimension'. How well-founded is the charge?

Not at all. Talk of a Turkish-supported 'Islamic arc' in the Balkans stretching from Bosnia across the Albanian ethnic space and reaching into Bulgaria's Turkish minority region and Greece's Western Thrace is in reality a propaganda concept promoted by Belgrade as a justification for Serbia's anti-Albanian and anti-Bosnian Muslim policies. It also enjoys much support in Greece because of its anti-Turkish and anti-Albanian connotations. In reality, there is little that binds those very diverse groups together. Islam is a link only in a formal sense. The Albanians, though largely Muslim, are not particularly religious. Nor are the Bulgarian Turks. Nor were, to begin with, Bosnia's extremely secularized Sunni Muslims who have, however, become more radicalized as a result of the Serbian aggression against them. The 'Islamic factor' is unlikely to assume a major importance in the Balkans but if it should do so, this will be directly attributable to actions that have little or nothing to do with religion and everything to do with political and military leaders posing as 'Christians'. If this should happen, nobody would be more dismayed than Turkey's firmly secular government, which sees Islamic militancy abroad as well as at home as a direct threat to itself.

States usually cooperate and unite in common action not only for positive but also for negative reasons – against somebody or for want of opportunity of joining a better club. Every ex-communist state in the Balkans wants to 'join Europe' – just as the ex-communist states further north do. But the wait for full membership of the European Union could be very long. Meanwhile, there could be disappointment with the norms of today – full free-marketry and political pluralism – and a search for different formulas. The good thing about such groupings as might be emerging in the Balkans now is that they would be flexible enough to fulfil many different purposes and roles for their various members.

Realistically speaking, the *Kleinmitteleuropa* grouping could link its members more closely to 'Europe' but it could also provide reassurance against both future German hegemony in the north and possible local irredentist moves from, say, Italy in the west and Serbia's expansionism in the east. Last but not least, it could help to deter a resurgent Russia from trying to muscle in on the region. A Balkan confederation could, in a sense, do even more. Psychologically, it could offer its more defensively-minded members a measure of reassurance against both Catholicism and Islam (defined as broad politico-religious tendencies). More specifically, Serbia, exhausted by its wars in Croatia and Bosnia, might feel reassured about what is these days seen among the Serbs as the Albanian demographic wave rolling northwards and 'engulfing' their country. Bulgaria, Greece and Serbia would be able, within such a framework, to accept a separate Macedonia. For both Greece and Bulgaria, there would be an additional reassurance in such company against fears of Turkish hegemony over the region. (Such fears, including current talk in Greece of a 'hundred million strong neo-Ottoman Islamic empire', are wildly unrealistic, but *Angst* is the stuff of politics in the Balkans as much as elsewhere.) As far as Romania is concerned, membership of such a Balkan grouping would take it out of its isolation from its neighbours and the rest of Europe and, very important, prevent over-dependence on Russia. The Turkish scheme for Black Sea Cooperation, taking in all the states concerned – Azerbaijan, Bulgaria, Georgia, Moldova, Romania, Russia and Ukraine as well as of course Turkey itself – and signed in July 1991, is partly designed to allay the mutual fears of these states.

Kleinmitteleuropa and a Balkan confederation: a speculative scheme, admittedly, but perhaps with more realism in it than some of the more backward-looking schemes lingering here and there and envisaging, for example, the reconstruction of Yugoslavia. And if it resembles the pattern of those pre-1914 alliances, then it does so only very superficially and with one vital difference: because of the strategic downgrading of the Balkans, there is, fortunately, little danger this time of a third world war; but also, regrettably, there can be no promise of local harmony either. The best that can be hoped for is that the emerging groupings will provide enough flexibility to contain and neutralize the region's old and new tensions alike.

Im Balkan viel Neues. Things have certainly changed in the Balkans, but have they changed for the better? The post-communist order is still in the making but there is no need to cry for the *Pax Sovietica*, a lost half-century for the region. Even though the ugly and barbaric practice of 'ethnic cleansing' has, regrettably, been recently revived by the Serbs, in general acquisition of territory has ceased to be the consuming preoccupation it once was. Good economic performance is appreciated as what makes states strong and stable. Although former Yugoslavia's acceptance of that principle must await the resolution of the current extremely messy and bloody reordering process, it is a principle that is coming to be understood by the new post-communist leaders, as well as their peoples, and will perhaps in the end encourage cooperation rather than irredentist wars in the region.

Notes

1 For a treatment of Turkey as a Middle Eastern power, see Philip Robins, *Turkey and the Middle East* (Chatham House Papers, RIIA/Pinter, May 1991). See also Gareth Winrow, *Turkey in Post-Soviet Central Asia* (London: RIIA, 1995).

2 For an analysis of the dramatic changes since West European integration was launched, and a consideration of future trends in Europe as a whole, see William Wallace, *The Transformation of Western Europe* (London: RIIA/Pinter, 1990). An assessment of the political and economic changes in Central Europe in 1989–90 and the process that preceded it can be found in Judy Batt, *East Central Europe from Reform to Transformation* (London: RIIA/Pinter, 1991). John Pinder, in *The European Community and Eastern Europe* (London: RIIA/Pinter, 1991), charts the evolution of the European Community's policy towards Central and Eastern Europe and examines some of the serious dilemmas facing it in the area.

3 Karl Marx and Friedrich Engels, *Manifesto of the Communist Party*, English translation annotated by Friedrich Engels (New York: International Publishers, 1932), p. 28.

4 V. I. Lenin, 'Critical Remarks on the National Question', in *Questions of National Policy and Proletarian Internationalism* (Moscow: Progress Books, n.d.), p. 30.

5 Svetozar Vukmanovic-Tempo, *Revolucija koja tece: Memoari* (Belgrade: Komunist, 1971), vol. I, p. 30.

6 For a full and authoritative account of Albanian conflicts during the Second World War, see Sir Reginald Hibbert, *The Bitter Victory: Albania's National Liberation Struggle* (London: Pinter, 1991). The author was in Albania during the war as an officer working for the Special Operations Executive (SOE).

7 The extremely complex and controversial question of the exact number of people – Serbs, Croats, Jews, Muslims and others – killed in Yugoslavia during the Second World War is treated seriously and with remarkable

129

objectivity in two studies, one by a Serb and one by a Croat. The Serb author, who has lived in the West for many years, is Bogoljub Kocovic. His book, published by *Nasa Rec*, a Serbian monthly, in London in 1985, is called *Zrtve drugog svetskog rata u Jugoslaviji* ('Victims of the Second World War in Yugoslavia'). The author of the other study, called *Gubici stanovnistva u drugom svjetskom ratu* ('Losses of the Population of Yugoslavia in the Second World War'), is a population expert, Professor Vladimir Zerjavic. His study was published in Zagreb by the Yugosav Victimological Society with the support of the Jewish community in Zagreb. Both Kocovic and Zerjavic come to remarkably similar conclusions, even though they carried out their research independently of each other. Both state that the actual figure was lower than is commonly assumed.

8 For the 'revisionist', pro-Mihailovic view, see Michael Lees, *The Rape of Serbia: The British Role in Tito's Grab for Power 1943–1944* (New York: Harcourt Brace Jovanovich, 1990); and David Martin, *The Web of Disinformation: Churchill's Yugoslav Blunder* (New York: Harcourt Brace Jovanovich, 1990). Still the best scholarly work on Mihailovic's movement is Jozo Tomasevich, *The Chetniks* (Stanford, CA: Stanford University Press, 1975).

9 See Richard Crampton, *A Short History of Modern Bulgaria* (Cambridge: Cambridge University Press, 1987), pp. 148–9.

10 That understanding, scribbled on a piece of paper by Churchill and ticked by Stalin, gave the Soviet Union a 90% stake in Romania and 75% in Bulgaria, while Britain (and the West in general) got 90% in Greece. Each side received a 50% stake in Hungary and in Yugoslavia. See Winston Churchill, *The Second World War, Vol. 11: The Tide of Victory* (London: Cassell, 1954, paperback edition 1964), pp. 200–201.

11 For a fuller treatment of the competing railways question, see Orme Wilson Jr., 'The Belgrade-Bar Railway: An Essay in Economic and Political Geography', in George W. Hoffman, ed., *Eastern Europe: Essays in Geographical Problems* (London: Methuen, 1971), pp. 365–94.

12 Much has been written on the subject of Yugoslav self-management, most of it rather unilluminating or even positively misleading. One of the few who saw through the obfuscations was Ljubo Sirc in *The Yugoslav Economy under Self-Management* (London: Macmillan, 1979).

13 See Dusan Bilandzic, *Jugoslavija poslije Tita 1980–1985* (Zagreb: Globus, 1987).

14 The 1981 census figures mentioned in this chapter are available in *Statisticki godisnjak Jugoslavije 1988* (Belgrade: Savezni zavod za statistiku, 1988).

15 The first full published version of the Memorandum appeared in the Zagreb journal *Nase teme*, Nos. 1–2/1989. (A French translation is

available in a volume called *Le nettoyage ethnique. Documents historiques sur une idéologie serbe* edited by Mirko Grmek, Marc Gjidara and Neven Simac and published in Paris by Fayard in 1993.) A book that expresses the essence of Serbian feelings about Yugoslavia and the Serbs' position in it is Danko Popovic's best-seller *Knjiga o Milutinu* (Belgrade: Knjizevne Novine, 1985).

16 Branko Horvat, *Kosovsko pitanje* (Zagreb: Globus, 1988).

17 The Slovene declaration of independence ('Deklaracija ob neodvisnosti') was published in *Uradni list Republike Slovenije* (*Official Gazette of the Republic of Slovenia*), no. 1, 25 June 1991, pp. 4–5. English translation in *The Case of Slovenia* (Ljubljana: *Nova Revija*, 1991), p. 181.

18 Norman Cigar, 'The Serbo-Croatian War, 1991: Political and Military Dimensions', in *Journal of Strategic Studies*, vol. 16, no. 3, September 1993, pp. 297–338. (Norman Cigar is Professor of National Security Studies at the Marine Corps Command and Staff College, Quantico, VA.)

19 'Information Notes on Former Yugoslavia', no. 10/1994, October 1994 (UNHCR, Office of the Special Envoy for Former Yugoslavia), p. 18.

20 *Borba* (Belgrade), 11 July 1991.

Bibliographical note

It is not practicable in a short work such as this to provide more than a few references to sources used in the course of its preparation – let alone an exhaustive bibliography. But here are a few suggestions (to supplement those works cited in the Notes) for readers who may wish to explore further in works available in English certain of the themes covered.

An excellent, up-to-date historical survey, equipped with an extensive bibliography and index, is Richard Crampton's *Eastern Europe in the Twentieth Century* (London and New York: Routledge, 1994, 475 pages), which takes the reader right up to and beyond the 1989–91 revolutions. There are also two useful works, complementing each other, by Joseph Rothschild: *East Central Europe between the Two World Wars* (Seattle and London: University of Washington Press, 1974, 420 pages); and *Return to Diversity: A Political History of East Central Europe since World War II* (New York and Oxford: Oxford University Press, 1989, 257 pages). Another concise, useful work covering the recent history of the whole region, with particular emphasis on the 1918–41 period, is Antony Polonsky's *The Little Dictators: The History of Eastern Europe since 1918* (London and Boston: Routledge and Kegan Paul, 1975, 212 pages). For the earlier, imperial period, there is Alan Palmer's *The Decline and Fall of the Ottoman Empire* (London: Weidenfeld, 1993, 306 pages); and Alan Sked's *The Decline and Fall of the Habsburg Empire* (London: Longmans, 1989, 295 pages).

For a feel of what Europe – and Eastern Europe, in particular – was like and what its preoccupations were in the pre-communist era, it pays to dip into H. Hessell Tilman's *Peasant Europe* (London: Jarrolds, 1934, 282 pages). And, of course John Gunter's splendid *Inside Europe* (London: Hamish Hamilton, 1936; revised, illustrated edition 1937). In the section on Yugoslavia, for example, it reports that 'General Goering swooped on a few visits to Yugoslavia and pleased the boy King with a tremendous toy railway as a birthday gift'.

Specifically on the Balkans, there are two useful works: Barbara Jelavich's *History of the Balkans, Vol. 2: Twentieth Century* (Cambridge: Cambridge

University Press, 1984, 647 pages); and the volume edited by Charles and Barbara Jelavich, *The Balkans in Transition. Essays on the Development of Balkan Life and Politics since the Eighteenth Century* (Berkeley and Los Angeles: University of California Press, 1963, 451 pages). The often neglected but important economic angle is treated in a joint work by John R. Lampe and Marvin R. Jackson, *Balkan Economic History 1550–1950: From Imperial Borderlands to Developing Nations* (Bloomington: Indiana University Press, 1982, 728 pages). A useful volume looking at contemporary conflicts in the Balkans from a historical perspective is *Problems of Balkan Security: Southeastern Europe in the 1990s*, edited by Paul S. Shoup (Project Director: George W. Hoffman) and published by the Wilson Center Press in Washington in 1990. A highly topical, up-to-date treatement of the security angle is to be found in *The Volatile Powder Keg. Balkan Security after the Cold War*, edited by F. Stephen Larrabee (Washington: The American University Press, 1994, 320 pages).

The most acute and perceptive analysis of the relationship between communism and nationalism in the Balkans, still valid for its insights despite having been published two and a half decades ago, is Paul Lendvai's *Eagles in Cobwebs* (London: Macdonald, 1970, 396 pages). In the same category of works published long ago but still illuminating is Elisabeth Barker's short study *Macedonia: Its Place in Balkan Power Politics* (London: Royal Institute of International Affairs, 1950, reprinted 1980, 129 pages). Her *British Policy in South-Eastern Europe in the Second World War* (London and Basingstoke: Macmillan, 1976, 320 pages) is an account of the emergence of the post-1945 settlement in the region. Macedonia is also the subject of a joint work by Stephen E. Palmer Jr. and Robert R. King, *Yugoslav Communism and the Macedonian Question* (Hamden: Archon Books, 1971, 247 pages).

A helpful work providing a broader conceptual framework for thinking about nationalism is Anthony D. Smith's *National Identity* (Harmondsworth: Penguin Books, 1991, 227 pages). It is interesting to read it in conjunction with an early attempt to make sense of the whole problem of modern nationalism, a study compiled by a team at Chatham House in the 1930s under the chairmanship and direction of E. H. Carr. Its title was *Nationalism* and it was published by Oxford University Press for the RIIA in 1939.

The main historical Balkan disputes are treated in some detail in the Robert R. King's well-documented scholarly study *Minorities under Communism: Nationalities as a Source of Tension among Balkan Communist States* (Harvard: Harvard University Press, 1973). A detailed, up-to-date survey of the minorities issue is to be found in *The Balkans: Minorities and States in Conflict* by Hugh Poulton (London: Minority Rights Publications, 1991, 242 pages). A broader European policy perspective on the minorities issue is offered in *Minority Rights in Europe: The Scope for a Transnational Regime*, a Chatham House Paper edited by Hugh Miall (London: Pinter for the RIIA, 1994, 128 pages).

Albania. Solid historical background, with a sense of perspective, is to found in Anton Logoreci's *The Albanians: Europe's Forgotten Survivors* (London: Gollancz, 1977, 230 pages). Also useful for background is Peter R. Profti's *Socialist Albania since 1944: Domestic and Foreign Developments* (Cambridge, MA: The MIT Press, 1978, 311 pages). In *Albania's National Liberation Struggle: The Bitter Victory* (London: Pinter, 1991, 269 pages), Sir Reginald Hibbert provides a well-documented account, partly based on personal wartime experiences as a British officer, of Albania during the Italian and German occupation right up to the communist takeover. James Pettifer's *Albania* in the Blue Guide series (London: A & C Black; New York: W.W. Norton, 1994, 237 pages) combines historical and geographic background with up-to-date political and economic information. The same is true of Derek Hall's *Albania and the Albanians* (London: Pinter, 1994, 304 pages).

Bulgaria. The best overall study, concise and informative, is Richard Crampton's *A Short History of Modern Bulgaria* (Cambridge: Cambridge University Press, 1987, 221 pages). For the crucial early period of communist power, there is J.F. Brown's *Bulgaria under Communist Rule* (London: Praeger, 1970, 339 pages).

Romania. A gripping and, at the same time, most informative account of wartime Romania, based on personal experiences as a British agent there, is provided by Ivor Porter in *Operation Autonomous. With S.O.E in Wartime Romania* (London; Chatto & Windus, 1989, 268 pages). On the early communist period, there is Ghita Ionescu's *Communism in Rumania, 1944–1962* (London: Oxford University Press, 1964, 378 pages); and for the Ceausescu era, Michael Shafir's *Romania: Politics, Economics, Society Political Stagnation and Simulated Change* (London: Pinter, 1985, 232 pages).

Former Yugoslavia. The key work for understanding the whole of the Yugoslav problem is Ivo Banac's magnificent monograph *The National Question in Yugoslavia: Origins, History, Politics* (Ithaca and London: Cornell University Press, 1984, 452 pages). The importance of the 'national factor' within the Communist Party is one of the important themes also in his *With Stalin Against Tito: Cominformist Splits in Yugoslav Communism* (Ithaca and London: Cornell University Press, 1988, 294 pages). An earlier but still useful monograph on the same subject is Paul Shoup's *Communism and the Yugoslav National Question* (New York and London: Columbia Viking Press, 1968, 308 pages). A lucid, comprehensive survey of the Tito period from the pen of a shrewd contemporary observer is Sir Duncan Wilson's work *Tito's Yugoslavia* (Cambridge: Cambridge University Press, 1979, 269 pages). The most up-to-date and readable study of Tito which also, helpfully, covers the broader historical and international context is *Tito: A Biography* by Jasper Ridley (London: Constable, 1994, 495 pages). A handy, concise compendium is a volume originally prepared for the Naval Intelligence Division in London during the Second World War and updated and edited by Stephen Clissold, *A Short History of Yugoslavia: From Early Times to 1966* (Cambridge: Cambridge University Press, 1966, 279 pages). Stephen Clissold also edited a selection of documents, prefaced with a long, illuminating essay and called *Yugoslavia and the Soviet Union 1939–1973* (was published by Oxford University Press for the RIIA in 1975).

Yugoslavia's violent break-up and the subsequent wars in Slovenia, Croatia and Bosnia are covered in many books – some informative, others less so. The most intelligent analysis of the conflicts that destroyed Tito's federation is to be found in Branka Magas's *The Destruction of Yugoslavia: Tracking the Break-up 1980–92* (London: Verso, 1993, 366 pages). The Yugoslav People's Army's role in the crises of the 1980s right up to Yugoslavia's break-up in 1991 is dealt with in *Legitimacy and the Military: The Yugoslav Crisis* by James Gow (London: Pinter, 1992, 208 pages). An intelligent and perceptive 'insider' account of the break-up is *The Yugoslav Drama* by Mihailo Crnobrnja, a senior Serbian official of the former Yugoslav government (London and New York: I.B. Tauris, 1994, 282 pages). Very useful both for its potrayal of the internal conflicts leading up to the war and of the wider international diplomatic and political context is *Europe's Backyard War: The War in the Balkans* by Mark Almond (London: Heinemann, 1994, 432 pages). The role of the media in the preparation for the war and its prosecution is subjected to a detailed, critical analysis by Mark Thompson in *Forging War: The Media in Serbia, Croatia and Bosnia-Hercegovina* (London: Article 19 International Centre Against Censorship, 1994, 271 pages). Noel Malcolm's *Bosnia: A Short History* (London: Macmillan, 1994, 340 pages) is in a category of its own as an authoritative, masterly account covering earlier history as well as the contemporary scene right up to and including the present tragic war.

Among the plethora of shorter studies in English it is worth noting two particularly helpful ones from the Institute for Security Studies of the Western European Union in Paris, both published in the Chaillot Papers series in 1994. They are *Lessons of Yugoslavia* by Nicole Gnessotto and *The Implications of the Yugoslav Crisis for Western Europe's Foreign Relations*, with contributions by Pavel Baev, Ali Hillal Dessouki, F. Stephen Larrabee, Duygu Bazoglu Sezer and Monika Wohlfeld and edited by Matthias Jopp.

International reviews of the first edition

'A valuable contribution to the elucidation both of the immediate and of the more long-term causes of the bloodiest and most destructive crisis of contemporary Europe.'
Mondo Economico, Rome, October 1993

'Comprehensive and rigorous, Cviic's book provides an opportunity to understand what has happened and what will happen in the Balkans.'
Corriere del Ticino, June 1993

'*Remaking the Balkans* ... explains in 150 pages the historical background to the present crisis that is inflaming the Balkan region.'
Il Sabato, July 1993

'Cviic's little book ... offers an interesting and succinct survey which enables the reader rapidly to grasp the essential questions and problems relating to the Balkans in the "new world order".'
Etudes Internationales, Quebec

'... topical and up to date, it will be of significant interest to historians, political scientists, specialists in international relations and Balkans scholars. It has a solid factual base and is rich in documentary material. The author has a deep knowledge of Balkan problems, looking at them "from within".'
Mirovaya edonomika i mezhdunarodniye otnoshenia, Moscow

'Cviic is a master of his subject. The book has a wealth of information and a lot of apt analyses and comments.'
Slovenec-Ljubljana

'Christopher Cviic's book is an excellent guide to the complicated rules of the latest Big Game.'
The Tablet, London